No Air

Big girls don't cry
Part Two

Ivana Ivancakova

Published in 2023 by Ivana Ivancakova

© Copyright Ivana Ivancakova

ISBN: 978-1-913898-70-0

Also available as an ebook

Cover and Book interior design by
www.pixeltweakspublications.com

Cover Illustration by Alexandra Tarcinska

This book is dedicated to everyone experiencing domestic abuse, the survivors and those who have lost their lives.

Contents

Prologue

Going back to London was very stressful and emotional. I was returning to the place I called home, a place where I had lived for few years, where hard work, determination, and luck will help bring your dreams to reality.

Only there was a strange feeling in my belly while passing through security at the airport (can you blame me??). I was flying from the east of Slovakia when only a week previously a little military training incident put the country in the spotlight all over the world.

During a training exercise, an explosive had been randomly placed in a passenger's luggage as part of a sniffer dog effectiveness test. The dogs detected the test material. But then a security officer failed to remove it, and the bag was loaded onto a flight to Ireland. With security checks not generally performed for arrivals, the passenger arrived and took the bag to his home in Dublin. Three days later, the area surrounding the poor man's apartment was sealed off and evacuated while bomb disposal experts recovered the sample. The passenger was arrested but soon released without charge.

Of course, after I checked my suitcase in, security called me over. Only to find out the bag in question wasn't mine. Typical! I didn't find that funny at all. I knew my life would not be easy, and a new start was a new life and an opportunity to find happiness. I survived a French prison; if I can do that, I can do anything! Sometimes, you pay for your trusting, naïve personality and good heart because life will teach you lessons the hard way.

The moment we touched down at Luton airport, I had tears in my eyes - Just when I thought I would never cry again. London was just as expected at the end of January. A new chapter of my life started right there, only a decade later. Life brings you unique challenges and broken hearts. And following your heart sometimes costs you, be careful what you wish for.

I Am Back

It was late evening now. Slowly walking together, breathing cold air, I could feel warm tears falling down my cheeks. Those were happy tears. He was here next to me. All those months in the prison, I was praying to see him one more time.

Those first few days with John were so emotional. I don't think I had ever spent so much time talking to anyone. I wanted nothing more but to just find happiness.

Back in France, I realised that trying to prove that I can make it on top isn't the priority and not the happiness that I am looking for. I was looking for something special and real. Something that money can't buy, someone that makes me smile without even trying, someone that gives me butterflies in the stomach when you just simply know. Is this what everyone in the world is longing for?

* * *

I believe that in life you meet people for a reason. Some of them are there to teach you a lesson, to make you a stronger, better person. Some of them stay for a while, but only a very few of them stay for a lifetime. A genuine friendship, and a second family, people that can see you for who you are and not for what your social status or what bank account statement states.

I stayed for two days with John before moving to my friends further south. Blessed with very few of those kinds of friends in my life, I spent the first few months after returning to England with them. It's never easy to start again from whatever drama or trauma you are recovering from but it's made a little easier when you have the right people around you. My friend Jennifer is a supportive and wise woman I always listen to and Miranda is a very special person in my life, she is strong, with a big heart for the people she cares about.

This was quite an emotional time for me. It was proving difficult to adapt to normal life after prison. I realised that it would not be easy, but I survived in there and if I could do that I could do anything. I understand this is nothing to be proud of, and life will test you. This is no time to give up.

The next few months were busy. I guess I was trying to fix everything as soon as I could. Working with the girls in the pub, travelling up and down to London to see John and sometimes getting casting jobs here and there. Even that I wasn't sure about it, returning during fashion week, and the first time was at one of London's VIP clubs, I wasn't sure if I was ready to be back in that world, and hoped my anxiety wouldn't kick off.

This was a recovering part of my life when I needed to figure out what's next.

After returning to England, I had to deal with the French police officer who sent me love letters in prison. The secret admirer had turned into quite an obsessive one and had called several times whilst I was in Slovakia then tracked me back to England. He even visited London on one occasion for work and begged me to meet up with him. I wasn't able to meet him because I had a Casting job to do. Also, I had feelings for John so was in no hurry to see him again. I was grateful for the letters he sent me in Paris as they kept my spirits up. But he shouldn't have expected me to run to him when I got out from there. After this things started to turn nasty and following a few assaultive text messages from him, I snapped my sim card, smashed my phone and changed my number too, just in case. After that, he didn't track me again, as far as I am aware.

As months passed by, I was spending more time with John. Travelling to London as often as I could. He was funny, charming, positive, supportive. He was my best friend.

Moving On

Hi Ivus, is there any chance you will be home for Christmas this year?

An unexpected email landed in my inbox. It was lovely to hear from my lovely best friend/cousin Dana.

She continued...

There is someone that would love to meet you. Remember, I told you I would show your diary to someone? I have news. Let me know as soon as possible! All good here will be nice to see you. Stay with us, then we can travel together back home for Christmas. Love Dana.

To avoid going crazy in prison, and also kill the time I wrote a diary ...plus I kind of read all the books that they had in the prison library anyway so it gave me something to do. I gave Dana the diary to read it and it sounds like she has passed it on to someone who would be able to help me publish it.

I hit a reply button. Guess I am going home for Christmas then.

I asked John "Babes, did you read that handwriting notebook, the one I left here with you?"

"Do you mean that one with 50 Cent and Victoria Beckham pictures stick on the front?"

"Yes, that one"

"Ahh No not yet, sorry I didn't have time Darling, Why?"

"Never mind, I just wanted to know that. Do you think that's all; I am going home for Christmas. My cousin set some kind of meeting with a publisher or someone that has read my diary".

"You have never said you want to publish that as a book?"

"Well no not really, because I never thought anyone would want to read it. You know how I feel about my dyslexia. I don't talk about it. It's like my brain switches off sometimes, especially when under pressure or stress. I write for me to get it out of my system just like the therapy".

"I should read it. I promise I will find the time, babes."

"Yes, that would be nice. I mean, your honest opinion will mean the world to me."

After a few conversations, we agree maybe we should live together after the new year. So when I return from Slovakia, I will just move in.

Very excited now, looking forward to spending Christmas and New year with my family, Dana has organised the meeting in Slovakia and moving in with John. Far too excited now, but I had to find some kind of temporary job as soon as I move in. My modelling and styling career is not going that well, yet ... I always believe if you work hard, follow your dreams, and never give up, there is no reason you shouldn't achieve your goals. And don't let people say you can't do it!

* * *

Dana was waiting at the airport on a lovely late December day. It was cold with winter sunshine touching your skin, not much snow yet, but hopefully by Christmas day there would be a little more. When I was growing up, we had very different winters. Spending time at the grandparents', back then the snow would be sometimes a few meters in height, and no school! Such childhood memories are my treasure.

Bratislava was beautiful, especially when spending time with your super organised cousin.

The meeting that she had set up, turned out to be with a quite successful publishing house, well known for publishing books based on real-life stories. Meeting with the owner herself an author too was like meeting a Miranda (from The Devil Wears Prada) in the Slovak book world. When we finally left the publishing house office, I had the signed book contract in my handbag and book due out in the bookstores and online for March.

To be fair, since I moved to England a few years earlier, I hardly visited or kept up with media, and celebrities back home. I wasn't being ignorant, I was quite happy with the old school classics that I grew up with.

Next day we had a lovely train journey across the country to get back home for Christmas. Back to our simple home village, to spend this special time of the year with love ones. I will have to find the right time to break the big news. I just signed a contract with Pink publishing and my book will be out in just three months. Before the launch there will be a huge media promotion which will mean talking about the Paris issues. My parents will not feel too happy about this.

The festive season spent with my parents and my little brother was a bit more special this time, as we all were home together for the holiday. The supreme gift for my parents was to have both children back home together and seeing them happy, me not looking anorexic, and being more social was probably the best present for them all.

I have full support from them about the book. For me, it was a very emotional time as looking years back, I never thought I would have Christmas with family or even hope to see them. The Paris trauma stayed for a while with me. There were good days and there were bad. I learn to deal with it in my way, which was work, writing notes, keep telling yourself, if you manage there somehow you can do anything, I am so blessed and great full for being alive and mentally all right with no pills. I always believed there is a reason for everything in life and someone up there is monitoring you. (meaning God)

Silvester and New year was just like every other year with my parents and neighbours and the rest of the family living in the village. I was always quite happy to watch a television set and eating homemade cakes with a glass of Martini. I am not a big fan of the fireworks so do dog and rest off the animals.

Holiday Christmas break ends, and I was so excited to go back home to London to my man. Missing John a little too much now. It is a new year with a lot of fresh adventures together. I will be back in Bratislava only in a few months for the Promo of my book. I can't even believe this is happening.

John's reaction to my big news was, "Wow, babes, didn't see that one coming. Congratulations, now I will have to read that diary".

My life was moving on in a happy and positive direction now, so I learned how to focus on being around people again. My confidence still wasn't at100% and I had flashbacks from Paris. Airports still freaked me out and only travel only with hand baggage in the future. I do strictly no shopping in markets, no goods without a receipt, no helping strangers with their bags anywhere at airports and stations of any kind... I definitely learned that lesson the hard way!

Back in London, moving in with John was a tremendous step and commitment. I loved every minute. The feeling when you just look at each other and you know exactly what you are both thinking, made you laugh without trying, those little things in life that mean the world to some of us. Pure happiness. And I found it with him, I felt so blessed and finally happy.

I was so in love and happiness positively affects us when we are love. I was loving the idea of living with my boyfriend, I guess when you pass the honeymoon stage; you find out annoying parts as well. But this time was still the honeymoon period, when everything was just about perfect, if you can call it perfect. Theoretically, no relationship is perfect.

Whilst searching for my ideal job, I find a temporary one in a Lebanese restaurant which was fun. I was still doing casting jobs here and there, and job interviews, and getting the book promotion ready in Slovakia. John and I were now spending every free minute together, cooking, shopping and picnics in Battersea park, which became one of my favourite places in London.

During this time, John slowly managed to get me on his personal trainer eating habits. I learned how to eat balanced meals and swap a few things in the kitchen so I didn't starve myself. But I could never give up my sweet tooth. It is impossible to give up chocolate! I can honestly say I had everything I could wish for. John has been an amazing best friend and partner, supportive, caring, and fun.

Weeks went by and it was nearly time for me to get on that flight to Bratislava for my book launch.

This was a very exciting project for me. The book was already out online, available to pre-order. And I was looking forward to holding my very own copy of the book in my hands. John was very supportive. I had little confidence after prison; it was still a work in progress. Anxiety will still kick off once in a while.

But on the positive side, I had survived Paris and I promised myself I would do anything after that experience.

Bratislava was lovely. I was staying in a hotel this time as my cousin Dana, was out of the city, which was fine. Anyway, she would be back the following evening. When we were growing up, Dana as my big cousin was the one that I would turn to with advice or girls talk. She was smart, independent, successful, and down to earth, an amazing person. And a good laugh. I look up to her and even years later I still llook forward to our girlie chats, and

I needed her support for this project. Honestly, I did not know the first thing about book promotion, chat shows, and radio interviews.

Was I ready for this? no not even close...

I was craving some Slovak sweets. It was a lovely evening in Bratislava, so I took a little walk around, trying to find a corner shop that would be still open in the evening. Sometimes I forget I am not in London. In the end, I return to my hotel empty-handed. Never mind, the walk was lovely and I will definitely have enough time to make up for all Slovak sweets and treats in the next couple of days.

My publisher and her team were well organised and had planned the next few days activities. This included book signing, television appearances, radio talk shows, and interviews. My cousin and I made some crazy memories during this time.

John checked on me every night, which was a kind of sweet and I loved it.. looking forward to the text messages every evening and every morning for him was lovely. I was very much in love.

After saying goodbye to my cousin at the train station, I boarded the overnight train to East Slovakia, I was looking forward to seeing my parents after such a busy few days.

I can honestly say sleeping on the train was an experience. People deserve a medal if they have a great night's sleep on them. I just couldn't get comfortable. The pillows were so hard my neck was killing me in the morning. I arrived at my parents' house very exhausted.

Headache from the train gone. Now I had to enjoy a few days with my parents and ignore the media. I planned to meet a few of my college friends for a drink in the town, after meeting with a local journalist.

Next day my Mum wakes me up with newspapers in her hands... "What is this?"

I could barely open my eyes and have no idea what she was talking about.

"Mum, it's a newspaper I guess?"

She was holding a few copies in her hands.

She said "I've bought all the papers that were left in the shop," and she passed me one.

Now I realised what she was on about. The picture was of me a few years ago on the cover of the newspaper showing off my tiny nipple.

"How did they get this?" Mum asked. She was clearly shocked and upset.

"Mum come on I, totally understand why you are upset, but I can't control this. It is not that bad? It's an old photo and my boobs are so tiny you can hardly see it, anyway"

"You got an answer for everything," she replied.

"Mum you have to look at things from a positive side. Things in life never go as you wish or plan so, it is what it is"

Not entirely sure, who I was trying to calm down, my mother or myself?

The little village had something to talk about now, not just my book and talk show appearances. It keeps the gossip going on until something more interesting pops up.

The small town still has its charm and feels like I have never left, but I also notice how much it has changed after all those years.

Walking down the high street lots of teenage memories pop up as I think of my college days and the daily train journey there. If only those old carriages could tell their stories. Mostly overcrowed with students you would meet all kinds of friends and groups that you would become part of.

My parents kind of get over the newspaper picture and John was very supportive of it. I enjoyed the time with family and friends before I returned home to London. Was I ready for all this book promotion and media stuff? No, I wasn't ready. I did quickly learn to have thick skin and ignore haters. With John's and my publisher's support, I learned to not let those things get to me. Even though it is not that easy, and I'm now not as surprised how many celebrities can't cope and go crazy. Anyway, it is a life lesson that you learn every day.

Back home I was enjoying happiness, life in London with someone that means more than the world to me. As months passed by, the book became the number one bestseller back home, which was amazing. I was very grateful for my cousin and her idea to approach the publishers.

Time spent with John was special. You know, like when at the end of a long day, there is someone waiting for you after work. This was a thrilling time in my life. I was always so excited to see him and knowing there was someone at home that loves me.

A few months later, I received a nomination for Best Author of the Year, alongside other writers from our publishing house and, of course, the rest of the country. It was just like a dream. I have always loved to read books, a lot of books, but few people knew I had dyslexia. I didn't feel comfortable talking about it, I simply just tried my best to ignore it or better say it, pretend that is not there.

To be nominated was a huge thing. Once again, I was off to Bratislava for the Best Author of the year Award, unfortunately without John as he had to work. My cousin Dana was there of course always to the rescue with all the information and updates about Slovak celebrities and gossip. As mentioned earlier. I am not up to date with any of that.

The event was fabulous, all set up in 1920s style. And no unfortunately, I didn't win, but honestly; I was just happy to be nominated and be able to attend the event with all the amazing and inspiring authors in the country.

When you live in London, life can get quite busy. You don't realise it, but all you do is work. It was summer already and once again I looked for some time off.

This time it was a visit to Prague, to promote my book over there for a few days and after that, a brief road trip with my brother back home to Slovakia to spend some quality time with our parents.

Happiness

I was exhausted. I hadn't had a day off in months. My thought was, 'well, it is work. I can't just say no'. I don't know how to say No. I should learn to say no! But I enjoy work, and being busy is so bad. It was a Saturday morning, and I was on my way to the studio as usual. I wasn't feeling my best, but again, I had been working so many hours. But something hadn't been quite right the last few days. I couldn't walk up the escalator or stairs without getting out of breath. I wondered if maybe I had asthma or if I was just overworked and needed to slow down a little.

Tomorrow would be Sunday, and I'd take the day off and rest; it's all good. The tube didn't make me feel so good, and why was I out of breath when walking up escalators? Jesus, I am so unfit I had to do exercise, seriously.

Never mind, coffee and blueberry muffin will fix this; everything will be fine.

Only until later in the day, whilst watching models practising, things somehow became blurry, and that's pretty much what I remember. I had fainted, and when I opened my eyes, worried faces stared at me.

I promised my studio team I would see a doctor and get myself checked. On the way home, I read a book on the tube as usual, but that day it gave me a headache, which was strange. Passing by the Boots store at Clapham Junction station, I could hear Nicole's voice in my head, 'maybe you pregnant,' and wondered if I should call in and get a pregnancy test. Silly me, I thought that would be impossible; the doctor had confirmed that already. But what if...

I was told I couldn't have children. Or if I were to conceive, it would take a long time, maybe never because of my past problems with anorexia and the fact that I had had an implant for many years.

We were kind of thinking about it a few months earlier, so I went to see the doctor. John pointed out to me that I am not a family person and that all I do is work. This wasn't the truth, of course. I wanted a family, but I wanted a security plan first and to organise the future and everything that comes with it. So there would be a plan and try to stick to it, and then life becomes less stressful.

Staring at the range of pregnancy tests through my massive Karl Lagerfeld shades, I do not know which is the most effective or bestselling. After a good fifteen minutes of staring, I ended up with one of the most expensive ones, one of just the regular ones, and one of the cheapest!

Back home, sitting on the toilet waiting for the results felt like time had stopped. I used all the sticks to get a definite answer. I finally looked at the first stick ... I saw a cross; the result was obvious. And the next one too. I am pregnant! Oh my god, I am pregnant! How is this possible? Tears poured down my face whilst I tried to reread the instructions just to make sure I'd read them correctly.

And, just at that moment, the front door opened.

John walked into the flat and saw me crying in the bathroom (our studio apartment was tiny. If you've ever lived in London, you know what I am talking about).

"What's happened? Why are you crying, babes?"

Without speaking, I just passed him a pregnancy stick.

He smiled. "Babes, but I thought you couldn't have kids? How? This is amazing."

"I know. I do not know how; just a few months ago, the doctor said I can't have kids, and I am not sure why I am crying."

John has a sparkle in his eyes. He looked so happy. I was smiling, crying, and terrified of even the thought of giving birth. This made sense why I was feeling so funny the last few weeks. It wasn't because of overworking or getting older; I was just pregnant. Were these mixed feelings of shock, excitement, happiness, worries, and maybe a bit of anger with my doctor for telling me differently?

It's understandable to feel a mix of emotions. Excitement, joy, and anticipation are all common feelings. It's normal to feel overwhelmed by the idea of giving birth, but focusing on the positive aspects of parenthood helped to ease my worries. Becoming a parent is a journey, and feeling many emotions along the way is okay. I just kept thinking about this wonderful little angel that will be a bit like me and a bit like a daddy and just how amazing it is to become a mummy and hold the little one in my arms.

I needed to tell my mum straight away. She would be so happy knowing and with the thoughts of becoming a grandma.

I reached for my phone, trying to figure out how to tell her. Usually, I wouldn't call that late in the evening so she may not panic, thinking something terrible had happened.

Mum answered.

"Hi mum, sorry to call so late. Were you asleep?"

"No, not yet, but is everything okay? You're calling late. You work all the time and find time to relax. Did you just come back from work?"

"Mum, everything is great. I am working a lot, but that's okay; yes, it exhausted me the last few weeks, but now I know why. I have something exciting to tell you."

"Are you coming home for Christmas?"

"No, mum, not that. Maybe you should sit down. I don't know how to tell you this. I am far too excited, and I need to tell you straight away. You are going to be a Grandma mum. I am pregnant."

There was silence on the other end.

"Mum, are you okay? Are you crying, mum?"

"I am here. Yes, I am crying happy tears. Are you sure? Did you see a doctor?"

"No, I didn't see the doctor yet. I have done a few tests, and it's a straightforward answer. I am pregnant. That explains why I felt so tired and strange for the last few weeks, out of breath. Everything and everyone smells to me."

"Well, you still need to see a doctor. I am so excited now, and your dad would be so happy to hear the news.

We thought we would never see grandchildren. Now you have to take it easy with work, eat well and make sure you research the essential things to do to stay healthy. You know you are not that young. And how is John? Did you tell him? Are you going to get married? Do I have to tell your brother? have you told him yet? Did you tell him before me?

I said, "Mum, please calm down a little, I understand you are overwhelmed, but you had to calm yourself down. Of course, John knows he is thrilled and excited. No, there are no plans for a wedding just yet; NOOO. And no, I didn't tell anyone yet. You are the first mum, and I would prefer to tell my brother by myself, if you don't mind.

"Well, all right then, I will tell your father, and you tell your brother."

That night I wasn't able to sleep. I was far too excited. I am going to be a mummy! I would love a little girl ... or boy ... well, girl or it doesn't matter. The important thing is that the child is healthy and has a happy, loving family. Smiling and staring at John, sleeping happily beside me, we would soon have our own family. A little angel that would be ours. I couldn't have wished for more. John was sleeping peacefully, and I loved watching him sleep and kissing him on the hair while he slept.

Mum asked when we were going to get married. God, I didn't think of that yet. I was never much of a traditional girl in this way. People can have happy lives together even without marriage. After all, it is just a piece of paper that shows legally that you belong to someone.

On the flip side, every girl loves to dream about the perfect wedding – the beautiful dress and how your man looks at you the way no one ever will when you walk down the aisle. Your eyes would say everything you need to know without saying one word. And what if he is not really up to this kind of commitment? What if he changed his mind? What if he leaves us? And I have to stay alone with the baby. No, stop that now! I was overthinking everything again. Stop that. Just look at him. Look how happy he is. There is no way he would do something like that. He said he wanted a family.

It must be the hormones or something. What's wrong with me? Why am I thinking like that? I need to calm down! I am far too excited, scared, and overthinking everything. I had to get some sleep now. Especially now, the baby needs to rest.

* * *

I sat at the doctor's and nervously flipped through a magazine, trying to keep calm. 'It's just a needle and a bit of blood, I thought, come on, get over it. How can you give birth to this baby if you fear needles? You can do this if you survived a Paris prison. You can do anything, remember?

I have had morning sickness for the whole day, not just the morning. I work out that if I suck on sweetie and drink water, it gets rid of the sickness feeling for a little while. Then it returns urgggg. I read online that this is normal, and the morning sickness should stop after a couple of weeks.

Thank God I had a friendly nurse who knew how to deal with white-coat phobia patients. She was simply amazing. She kept chatting, asking about my day and about being a first-time mum, so I didn't even know when she put the needle in; In no time, it was all done.

I left the surgery feeling great. I faced my fear. It's understandable to feel some anxiety about giving birth, but many women have successfully given birth, and I can too. I need to look into prenatal classes and support groups to help me prepare for the experience. But it's important to stay positive and take care of myself physically and mentally during this exciting time. Everything is perfect. I am going to be a mummy.

I was feeling a little obsessed about motherhood. I got all the information that I should know: healthy eating, vitamins, no more high heels, plenty of exercise, drinking a lot of water, moving as much as possible, and keeping working. I did the best I could to avoid buying clothes and baby essentials as it was far too early for any of that. Even though it is hard not to, those tiny outfits are too cute. Imagine our little angel in that dress. Ahh, she would be the cuties. (we don't know the gender yet, but I think it is a girl).

Thanks to my never-ending morning sickness, I had to stop using the tube to get to work. I carried my water bottle and sweets to suck on wherever I went. Oh god, I felt just like my grandma when she used to get those mints out of her pocket every time I was in church with her.

Great, I've turned into a 70-year-old granny looking for mints every time I feel sick (which was most of the day). Sometimes, I would have to get off the bus because I simply couldn't cope with some body odour, cigarette smoke or one of the many other smells you get standing in close proximity to commuters.

Acts of kindness and chivalry are becoming increasingly rare on public transport. I had to tell myself to remember that while some individuals may not offer their seat or extend a kind gesture, there are still many people who are kind and considerate.

I tried not to let the actions of a few individuals get me down. There are still many kind and considerate people in the world, and it's essential to focus on the positive interactions and experiences I have.

There were days when I was simply far too emotional about everything. I was doing my best to manage as normally as possible, even though I wasn't feeling it at all.

But there is no other way than just getting on with it and doing our best for what is best for ourselves. Not what other people try to tell you. Thank you for your opinion and advice, but I am not considering taking time from work; no, maybe slow down a little, yes. I couldn't possibly think why I would have stopped working. Who would pay the bills? Plus, I would go crazy if I had to stay home.

I didn't enjoy being pregnant as much as I thought. People would say, 'You are glowing' and look fabulous.' But all I felt was exhaustion from throwing up and peeing every few minutes! And, of course, I was always eating everything that smelled good and tasted good.

Soon we were on our way to the Westminster and Chelsea hospital for a very important scan.

Today is the day when we will find out the baby's gender.

I couldn't wait, even though I kind of already knew it was a girl, I can't explain why or how, but I simply had a feeling.

John was excited, too, as far as I could tell.

He'd said he didn't have a preference, even though I could see in his eyes that he would love a baby boy.

In the consulting room, the baby was feeling a bit camera shy, and the doctor needed it to move to a different position, so I had to go outside, walk around the hallway for a while, and drink Lucozade.

Back inside the room, staring at the screen, the doctor pointed to the shapes on the screen. I tried to figure out what John and the doctor were looking at, and then I saw It was a girl, a healthy girl, all fingers, toes and everything!

I knew it was a girl! I'm crying now, happy tears. I still can't see much on that screen.

God, what kind of mother am I? I thought I couldn't see her until they gave us a sonogram photograph. I don't know if I was crying because I was happy it was a healthy girl or because I couldn't see her on the screen.

Besides the unpleasant side of the pregnancy, the baby was growing nicely, moving around and keeping mummy awake all night long. I talked to her all the time. John did, too; it was the sweetest thing ever, and he loved this time.

Naming a child is a massive responsibility. It's theirs for life, so picking the right one that both parents like is essential. So no pressure then! I loved wondering who she would look like, how her voice would sound and, of course, the name we would choose for her.

I couldn't wait to hold her and kiss her.

The date was getting closer. I decided not to take any classes or watch birthing videos or anything of that sort. I knew very well I would be worried and panic sleepless nights away. I was terrified of giving birth. I still did all the checkups and hospital visits and decided to deal with the rest when the time came.

I quickly learned that pregnancy is quite an enormous challenge for a relationship. My sleepless nights, hormones and the whole thing with pregnancy have led to unnecessary arguments. This could be partly due to the lack of space in our apartment. The shoebox style of London living is suitable for working individuals that just go home to sleep. They aren't designed for newborns... or heavily pregnant women. The baby would be keeping me up the whole night, moving and kicking, and, of course, Daddy found that a problem because he got disturbed too and couldn't get his beauty sleep. The reality of becoming a parent didn't just come with being so excited about the baby. Responsibility comes with that. Take care of the whole new life as, in my eyes, the baby has become priority number one, full stop.

So, one day when John told me he was looking to start University the following September, I wasn't impressed.

I asked him Now, Why Now? You couldn't pick a worse time. Couldn't you wait until the baby is a little older, when we settle into a bigger place when I can work full-time again after maternity leave? You should be focusing on your family and baby, not on yourself. We should be looking for a bigger flat, taking into consideration that I won't be able to work as much as I used to as a baby comes first. How will we afford to live with the added cost of having a baby if you think just of yourself and University? I don't understand why you would have made such an irresponsible and selfish decision at the most crucial time of your life.

It's Time

My last week at work was quite emotional, with a mix of feelings for an exciting time in my life. On one side, I would finally welcome and hold our little girl in my arms. On the other side, I was so terrified of giving birth. I kept telling myself not to think about it and deal with it when the time came!

There were now only three weeks to go, and I would be holding my little girl. My last working day would be the following Sunday at the styling job, and then I would take two weeks holiday to rest and make final preparations. Extra clothes, nappies, bottles, baby carrier, baby milk and bottle steriliser, and essentials for me as a mummy. The first-time mum's stress was high as I wanted what was best for the baby. I wanted to breastfeed but had nightmares that after the birth, I didn't have milk, and there wasn't any baby milk at home, and the baby was crying, starving hungry. I would wake up all sweaty. It was only a dream. What the hell was going on with me and these dreams? I needed to make doubly sure I organised everything! The hospital bag had been ready for a few weeks by then, just in case.

Saturday was my day off, so I looked forward to spending it with John. I did my best to take walks and drink water, listen to my man as a personal trainer, and make sure the whole birth would go smoothly and the baby girl was healthy. It was not so easy to walk anymore by then, and I might not have looked like one, but I felt like an elephant.

It was a lovely spring day. The sun was shining, and flowers were slowly coming out. It was one of those magical days, fresh air and walking in my favourite place, Battersea park—the perfect place to relax. I was hungry all the time by then and craving some chocolate cake. Well, a baby girl needs cake, right? The thing about being pregnant is if you are craving something, you must have it right at that moment, or you will burst into tears: God, those feelings and hormones.

I returned home after eating about ninety per cent of the chocolate cake myself (and not even feeling bad or ashamed about it). Then I snoozed off a little.

I woke up feeling wet. To my horror, I thought I had pee'd myself. Just lately, I was peeing every few minutes.

Oh no, I hadn't pee'd myself. My waters had broken! The greenish -yellowish coloured liquid made me panic.

I yelled, "Babes, it's time to get me a cab now!"

Nothing was hurting ... yet.

John was relaxing on the sofa and gave me a look that said, 'calm down, would you? You have two weeks left yet.' I was rushing around, trying to find something to wear and put shoes on. While he still did nothing. "Jesus Man," I said, "It's bloody time would you move and get a taxi."

Two minutes later, he was helping me down the stairs. The contractions and pain were indescribable and getting unbearable. Honestly, it's like hundred times worse than having a root canal done at the dentist.

I have no idea how we got into that taxi or how quickly we ended up at the hospital. I remember trying to get hold of my parents back home and cursing in all the languages I could scream out at this point.

We arrived early evening at the hospital, and our perfectly healthy and beautiful baby girl arrived just three hours later.

John had never left my side and held my hand throughout; even when my nails dug into his skin, he still didn't move, and I will be forever grateful to him for that.

When the nurse handed our little girl to me for the first time, the entire world just stopped. The crazy pain is quickly forgotten, tears rolling down my cheek as I hold my little angel, this perfect little girl, with tiny hands. We called her Joy because of the joy she brought us.

I can't stop staring at her. She must be so hungry, searching for my boobs right away. Not sure if this is normal or just that our little one is starving.

The nurse said, "It's time for you to get into the bathroom. I will help you whilst Daddy tries to dress the baby girl".

John's face was like, "Oh okay, I dress the tiny newborn baby???"

He didn't say a word when I returned from the bathroom with the nurse, but he had successfully dressed the baby in her white hospital outfit. She looked so adorable. Still trying to figure out how, but he did a great job. I was a little worried about dressing the baby. She was so tiny and precious that I was scared to hold her, let alone dress her. Of course, I had been an Au pair, but that was very different. Laura was a few months old before I started looking after her.

That night I felt exhausted; I'd just pushed a baby out of my body, so I was sleepy and sore. I couldn't sleep much while checking on the baby girl lying next to me. Even though I knew John was there too, somehow I couldn't sleep. Don't think he could either, in that armchair. Both of us watched our little girl sleeping sweetly. So perfect, so tiny, our little angel.

I'd sent a message to my parents with the joyful news that they were grandparents. When I called, they were not home. Dad was out celebrating his sixtieth birthday, and my next-door neighbour grandma had a birthday too. The entire street had a party going on. This was a small village country-style life.

Three days later, on a beautiful sunny morning, we could take our tiny princess home. Not the perfect home for a baby, but at least it was home. Joy looked so tiny in her car seat, I couldn't take my eyes off her. She was sleeping so peacefully; apparently, all kids love to sleep in the car.

I was happy to be home and hoping to get some sleep; maybe, even a little would do!

I was emotional because I didn't have family around me, but I had my friends, work colleagues and my Au pair family. Jennifer and the girls came to see us. It was so lovely to see them. However, deep inside, I couldn't help but feel horrible, disappointed, and sad because John wasn't making any effort. I wasn't expecting a ring or anything like that. Flowers with chocolate would have been lovely. Maybe I was just being silly, making a big deal from nothing. I am not one of those girls who needs baby showers, birthdays, weddings or any materialistic things to prove happiness and love. Still, a slight gesture would be nice and thoughtful. There were no visits from his family or friends, which was strange. Not sure even if there were any friends.

The next few days continued to be tough with sleepless nights, then long days with no rest. Based on the midwife's advice, I was breastfeeding and practising skin to skin routine. I couldn't even go to the toilet in peace. As soon as I put baby Joy down, even for a few seconds, she would cry her eyes out. And I couldn't bear to hear her crying in her tiny voice. Of course, I fully expected the role of motherhood wouldn't be easy, especially when you're a first-time mum… even with Au pair experience.

The lack of space in our tiny flat wasn't the place for a newborn child. It all got too much for me. From that frustration, I told John how I was feeling and that I was upset that he'd not even bothered to get me flowers after we came home from the hospital after I'd just given birth to your child. Tears were pouring down my face, so I was stunned to hear John's answer. "What did you expect, a medal? You are not the first woman to give birth to a child". This reply hurt me deeply.

And this was the first moment when have realised something was not quite right.

The weeks and months slowly passed, and nothing changed much, only me not caring how I looked or what I wore.

I was doing my best to be a good mum, trying my best to breastfeed. This was important for me. Even though I learnt the hard way. I endured testing times with biting and milk coming out anytime and anywhere. Oversize sunglasses were a crucial essential accessory to hide my tired eyes and, of course, the odd cup of strong coffee (not as much coffee as I would like, obviously, as I was breastfeeding). The baby carrier was brilliant for walks and shopping. The flat was madness, far too small and unsafe for the baby. When the health visitor came to visit or my friends from work called in, it quickly got overcrowded, and I nearly had to put the chair for them in the hallway or bathroom.

We were three floors up, so getting the pushchair down the stairs was a nightmare. There was always so much mess at the bottom of the stairs, building materials and whatever. Also, the dormer windows leaked when it rained above Joy's cot. John wasn't getting much sleep either; the moving plans weren't getting anywhere, and when I dared to ask him about it. He'd say he was on it.

Ultimately, I couldn't see any other option than to take little Joy and myself over for a brief holiday to her Slovak grandparents. And that was the best decision I made. After consulting with the health visitor and Daddy, it was the best option—fresh farm air and to see my parents. Who could finally enjoy meeting their first grandchild, and I could get much-needed mummy's help. I could go home for a little longer than a week or two for the first time in years. It was an excellent opportunity to enjoy some of my maternity time with little Joy and my parents.

All the arrangements were made, and the essentials were packed for a baby. Joy's health and travel documents were ready, and the internet was sorted at my parent's house so that we could Skype with daddy every day.

Slovakia

After an interesting flight with a newborn, we had a brief delay with my bags at check-in. I wasn't aware that my Vitamin C boosting serum needed to be tested. In the end, they gave me the cream back. When you only have around 3-4 hours of sleep between the crying and breastfeeding, a boosting cream is essential for tired and grumpy skin! Thank god for the baby carrier; I can't imagine how I would have managed the journey without it. I was grateful to a friendly air hostess who helped me with the baby and all my hand luggage.

* * *

My brother and my mum were waiting at the airport. Mum and I tried our best not to become too emotional.

Back home, at last, fresh air and peace. It was late August, and the only noises you would hear on our street were a tractor, my daddy or a neighbour fixing something around the house; our dog that is not used to seeing us, and sometimes the rooster crows too much, especially just when I'd finally got Joy to sleep (it's as if he knew). Ahh, well, you can't have everything. At least it is not non-stop London noise.

I forgot how much I loved the simple life in the countryside—being able to have Joy with me in the garden while sleeping in her baggy. I could work with her right there next to me in the vegetable field: no stress, no deadlines, no noise and a happy baby girl. I soon realised Joy really enjoyed being outdoors too. She would sleep in her pushchair outside but wouldn't sleep during the day if I put her in her cot.

Well, she is indeed my daughter, so it made sense. Doing any work around a country house and field garden is more therapeutic and relaxing, and it doesn't feel like work. It's different from stressed-out days in the city with deadlines and everyday work issues. So yes, I enjoyed harvest time, fixing and redecorating around the house when Joy was having her nap with her grandparents on duty. I enjoyed working outside, soaking in the fresh air, and all that moving around helped me to lose my post-baby weight. While working in the garden, I had the 'clever idea' to wrap my belly in cling film under my t-shirt. It's supposed to be a faster and more effective way to lose weight while doing your everyday household tasks, but instead, it just left me with spots all over my belly and back!

John was Skyping every day in the morning and evening, which was great. There was not much going on with the flat at this point. He was 'still working' on it.

While spending time with my family, I discovered that mum had some health problems she hadn't told me about. So being home with Joy was quite special for us all. It was good to get help with Joy. Weeks went by, and it was getting colder. It was the first time in many years that I was home at this time of the year: the first frost and snow. For the autumn harvest, getting the garden ready for winter, cosy walks in meadows, picking rosehips and mushrooms.

There were days when I would miss John so much, even though we would Skype twice daily. I also sent him lots of pictures and videos of our little princess. This situation wasn't ideal; unfortunately, I couldn't see a better solution at this point. I should have sorted out a bigger flat myself. John wasn't doing so well at it. My maternity leave would end in just a few months, and I would have to return to London and work. Our current living situation is not safe for the baby. In reality, John was more focused on his priorities, which were starting university rather than making his family number the one priority.

* * *

December arrived, and Christmas with my parents was the first Christmas for baby Joy.

I was getting into the festive mood. It had been a long time since I'd been at my parent's house for my birthday and the festive holiday season. I had nearly forgotten all the small village family traditions. Sometimes the busy city lifestyle makes you pay little attention to birthdays or Christmas when busy with work. Becoming a mother and parent put a new perspective on these traditions as those of our special memory-making times.

I always love being creative, but I have never been good at baking cookies and cakes. Ironically I have a sweet tooth. Anyone who knows me will tell you that Ivana loves cakes and chocolate. I adore flowers and making floral creations for the festive season. Simple, homemade, and special to me. I would pop out to the meadow and woods to collect pine cones, frozen rosehip branches and whatever else I could find.

I was trying to make this year more special as I knew it thrilled mum that she could have us home for a while, especially during the holiday season. She had had a challenging year with her health, and someone very special in the family was quite unwell. I was doing everything I could to make this difficult time a little better.

Unfortunately, the Christmas we all were looking to remember because we had our little Joy with us, in the end, was quite a difficult time, especially for my mum.

* * *

As the New Year arrived, we enjoyed the snow with little Joy and a vintage sledge. Joy didn't seem to care much about the snowman we built. She was more interested in trying to eat the snow and let me know every time I stopped pulling the sledge. I guess some of mummy's old stuff, up in the attic, comes to some use sometimes.

January and February were much colder than December. Compared to the winters in London, I forgot the freezing weather they had here. Spending time there in the snowy weather was great. Staring outside through frosty windows with a cup of warm rosehip tea in my hands and admiring the beautiful winter wonderland was very relaxing.

After talking to John about family and my mum going through difficult times, I decided to stay longer than initially planned.

Joy grew more every day, and she loved the space and fresh air. She had plenty of room and soon started to crawl with little giggles. I stressed and overreacted to every single potential danger of all kinds. Joy discovered the fun of opening drawers and taking everything out. It kept me on my toes when the little princess found the freedom to move around the place.

It was March by now, and mum wasn't really up to a birthday celebration. We can try our best to make things easier for her. The weather was getting warmer, and the sunshine felt good on the skin. The snow was melting away, and snowdrops were popping out from the ground. Mother nature was waking up. It was time for me to return to London.

Back home

I was soon passing by the Luton airport arrivals gates. Pushing Joy in her stroller and trying to manage all the rest of the luggage, I quickly scanned around, looking for daddy and finally looking forward to seeing my man. Even though I don't like to admit life's difficulties, I missed him. I know we speak a few times every day on Skype. Then I saw him walking toward us, looking handsome as always.

At least he does; on the other hand, mummy looks exhausted, face covered with oversized sunglasses—hands and shoulders full of luggage and on top of everything, desperately needing to use the bathroom.

We quickly follow up with hugs, kisses and chit-chat. I Loved moments like this when I saw how happy he was. Joy was enjoying the moment with her daddy too. Before we headed to the car, some essentials were needed, baby changing and toilets, a stop for coffee and baby feeding time.

On our way home, it made sense to stop by and say hello to the other grandma. I am sure she would love to see Joy. Even though I wasn't my best unfortunately, I suffered from car sickness. A little stopover at grandmas should make me feel better. A few mints and travel pills normally will do the trick.

To my horror, I was sick in the car on the way home. Not so glamorous, but thankfully Joy's nappy bags come in handy.

After all the travel drama, I looked forward to snuggling up on the sofa with my man and our princess Joy. I have missed him, his jokes and the way his face lights up when he smiles, his cooking and how he looks at me. You cherish and try to remember the little things that mean the world to you when times get challenging.

I hadn't dared to ask anything about the flat or any progress related to the subject. He mentioned nothing himself. No, not today. Let's just enjoy being together.

* * *

Joy's first birthday was approaching. I was getting a little excited even though I knew John would not care about any birthday celebration. I wanted to make it a little memorable as it is a special day. Joy will be a one-year-old. A big deal in my eyes; this was my only child's first birthday. The first birthday!

Joy was taking her first steps, getting up and walking around the flat. In reality, though, in our one-room studio flat, there wasn't that far for her to walk anyway. The honeymoon period of our reunion passed quickly, and reality kicked in as soon as I questioned things. Well, I will return to work soon, so the priority is to sort out the situation. How are we going to manage this as a couple? I can't go back to working the hours that I used to.

And there was no obvious answer to anything from John. When I asked if he preferred me to sort it out, he would reply, he is on it.

* * *

Joy's birthday arrived! It was a lovely sunny day, and she looked adorable in her white summer dress with a matching hairband. (I know white colours and toddlers is never a good idea). It was her first birthday, and I won't be worried if she got too messy. Joy enjoyed a play in Battersea park. We spent most of the day outside and had a lovely family lunch at the restaurant. Her very first birthday cake was waiting at home, which Joy had to explore, trying to figure out what it was and why her face was printed on it. Sticking her tiny little fingers and hands into the entire cake was something very new and fun to do.

Later we Skyped the grandparents in Slovakia while singing happy birthday. Even without having a family party for Joy with everyone around, it was quite a lovely day… until later hours that evening.

An argument with John about the flat accommodation and University started later that evening. He was still determined to start in September. He was still planning to cut his working hours. To me, this was not the right time. How is this a priority? Your family, your little girl, is a priority, not you, at this point. The bigger flat, working together as a team, parents, and partners so we can work our jobs around Joy and then when she is a little bigger, we can progress your dreams. Why now? The timing couldn't be worse!

I felt so worked up by the situation that I began hyper-ventilating and having a full-blown panic attack. I can't remember much more.

I awoke later in the hospital; the paramedics had been called and had taken me there in the ambulance. They told me the situation that had caused this panic attack was a red flag for domestic abuse. I guess they saw things I couldn't see until a few years later.

Three Years Later

Once again, I was grateful for my oversized sunglasses. They are not just for shelter from the sun or to cover tired mums' makeup-free face but also to cover the pain and bruises that no makeup can. I am hugging my beautiful girl, as she was chatting excitedly whilst watching the world passing by from the train window.

The day I will never forget was the 1st of May 2018. The day I finally took the first step to free myself from an abusive life and try to save whatever was left of it. Not only for me but primarily for my little girl for this little smile, for this incredible human being that didn't deserve to witness so much.

John had dropped Joy at the nursery that morning. I had left for work before then, as usual. With the help of my work colleagues, police and friends, we planned a safe way out. There was no time to explain to the nursery teacher why I was taking Joy earlier than usual. I only managed "Family emergency. I will call you in the next few days if that's okay". I was losing much more than the nursery Joy attended. Everyone was so lovely there. Finally, I can breathe a little now, and my whole body is in pain. I wasn't feeling much pain until I lifted Joy and tried to walk faster than usual.

Clapham Junction station is always busy, but it seems extra busier today. The ticket office and machine queues are much longer. My paranoia and anxiety kicked off. This whole situation was just like a movie scene. I imagined seeing John everywhere. What if he is not at the University? What if ...

* * *

Seeing my oldest friend Lesley waiting at the station was reassuring, although the circumstances weren't ideal. Last week I finally found the courage to pick up the phone at work and call Miranda. Tears poured down my face when I heard her voice; she once again told me she'd cover my messed-up arse. With no questions, "Just get your baby girl and come here", she said.

Never mind how many years pass by, there are very few people in my life to whom I will always be very grateful. Miranda wasn't my mum or blood relation of any kind. She was someone so special. A woman and human being that is very rare to find. People in life come and go; some of them teach you a lesson and make you who you are. Some of them stay only for a while, and very few of them are for a lifetime. You always have them in your heart, even if your life moves on. They become your family.

The local police arrived shortly. The London metropolitan police contacted them when my work colleagues got the news that I was safely on the train on my way. It was hard to control my emotions when I saw them again, with little Joy in my arms and massive sunglasses covering the bruises under my eyes.

As Joy was having fun with Miranda, Lesley and the rest of the family, the first steps of madness started for me. Those officers were the first ones to write a report. Someone will be coming tomorrow to take me to make a complete video statement. So I need to make sure Joy has a babysitter.

* * *

The next day I'm sitting in a room that looks like a typical living room at a secret location with cameras everywhere. Police officers were setting up the video statement.

So, Miss, just to be clear, when the camera is on, first we ask for all the essential and necessary information. I understand that this is difficult. You are still traumatised and stressed, but please try to remember all the pieces of information and events that you can in order. We can always update the information if you forget anything.

From what I understand, this is not one event but concerns a few years of abuse, so don't worry if you can't recall everything. We work with these types of cases all the time; here is a glass of water and tissues. I'll stop you if I need to ask any questions. Are we ready?

I felt sick in my stomach; it was impossible to stop the emotions and tears no matter how hard I tried. I kept telling myself, 'I have to do this. I have taken the first step for Joy and me. This is the right thing to do. I was giving in to him too much; it would not improve. I tried the best I could to save our family to help him.

My name is Ivana Ivancakova, and I am a long-time partner of John James, biological father to our only daughter, Joy. We met in Stratford in the autumn of 2008 and have lived together in south London since January 2011.

John became my best friend and rock, the one to whom I would always turn. He was kind, funny, and someone I believed I would spend the rest of my life with. I used to love to make him smile with little things. He was my entire world. Those were a happy few years when I used to rush home from work so we could spend time together. For the last few years, I was rushing home from work with a sick feeling in my stomach because I wasn't sure what mood I would find him in. If I were late, he would text me nasty messages.

So when did the abuse start? When did he change?'

After Joy was born, there was a problem with our tiny flat and my opinion on his decisions. He put himself first, not the family. After Joy was born, he packed in his job, went to University and worked part-time. I wasn't able to work full-time anymore. I needed to look after Joy.

For the last three years, I have been working three days a week packed while Joy was at the nursery. I would look after Joy and the household the rest of the week and translate and publish my original book.

If ever I mentioned getting more working hours or an extra day to progress in my job for a better wage, John's answer would always be the same 'I don't have time for your bullshit'. By then, I wasn't even sure he was still working part-time. He'd hardly left the flat in the past few months. I didn't do any modelling anymore. Since having Joy, I have only done a couple of projects. I'd had to ask John for permission to do those, which he gave after checking on the entire team involved, and he would be okay to look after Joy for a day.

This photo shoot would be the first one in a long time. Because it was shortly after my birthday, it would be lovely to have a day to myself, do something like a hobby, and enjoy and relax creatively. Lots has changed since having Joy, and there was no time for me to have any 'fashion creative time' and no support from John. So the photo shoot was booked, and I looked forward to spending some 'me time'.

Just a day before the shoot, John told me he had exams and had no time to help with Joy after all. Really? A day before the shoot, he told me this. So I had to sort it out with the nursery myself. And, of course, a few days later, I found out John had no exams that day.

On another occasion, I had arranged to do a promotional video shoot for my book with a Slovak fashion designer and his partner. They were close friends who John had met and knew. Once again, I had to ask for his permission, as ideally, we wanted to get ready in our flat and then do the video shoot at Battersea park. John was initially okay with the idea until the day of the shoot arrived. Two hours before everyone was due, John went crazy mad, calling me all kinds of names, saying that I was so irresponsible to let strangers in the flat, also people from 'my country'. I cried and begged him on my knees to stop doing this to me; it was stressful and made me seem unprofessional. When my friends arrived, they knew something was wrong, but we still made the video. John didn't go to University as usual. The atmosphere in the flat was toxic. John could have been more friendly. I asked if he would like to come along with us and help with Joy. He didn't want to do any of that. Joy was happy with us in her pushchair on set, having fun. This was the last time I got involved in anything related to my hobbies or interests. John was very controlling, verbally abusive, selfish, and paranoid. After everyone left the flat, he wiped the whole leather sofa with antibacterial wipes because the boys (the designer and his partner) had been sitting there. I felt physically sick.

After this, things went from bad to worse. When I launched my self-published book here in London, he went mad once again because I was talking outside with the boys (same designer and his partner), and he now created the idea in his head that I was having an intimate relationship with them, even though they are gay.

John called me names more and more often and kept being suspicious of me cheating with people from work and even the postman and the builders working outside the flat. Basically, if I said 'good morning' or even talked to someone I met, he went mad. Abusive calls and texts from him became a regular thing while I was at work. He was home most of the time and I was working or looking after Joy. I would take Joy to Battersea park or go out food shopping. Occasionally I would meet with one of my three girlfriends in the park. I couldn't always invite them to the flat as John would be home. Those were the only girls that I would invite around to our apartment.

Let me stop you here, so you didn't have friends or family visiting you? How about his family?

Well, no, not really. He would not be happy with having visitors around our home. His family wasn't involved. He kept Joy and me away from them as much as he could. I saw his mum and sisters maybe four or five times in our ten years together. When I gave his family our address, he went mad at me and called me a snake. He wouldn't let me meet with his mum so she could get to know Joy. His mum visited once.

Then the abuse started, not just mentally, but physically. From arguments and shouting to slapping and spitting in my face, and once even pouring water on me while I had Joy in my arms, lots of this behaviour happened in the last few years.'

Tears poured down my face. I couldn't remember everything; it was like flashbacks, my sad, lonely memories, but not always in the correct order. I am so sorry I said. I can't stop crying. Can I have a drink of water, please?

Don't worry, have a drink, try your best, don't worry, whatever you forget, we will go over. I understand this is difficult for you. Do you recall the first event, when it was more physical, and slowly try to go until the last one? Can you do this?

'Yes, I will; well, I can' as I nod.

Things went worse since he went to University. At first, it was normal, then slowly got worse and worse. It gradually got worse, and saying things like, 'you think you are better than me?' when I tried to give my opinion, he would tell me I was not educated enough to comment. On top of this, I was stupid, not fit to be a mother, mentally ill, and a paedophile. He called me all kinds of names … Eastern European whore, prostitute, white trash, farm girl.

He would wake me up at 2-3 am by taking the blanket off me and beating me up, slapping me on the face saying, "You think I would let you take Joy with you? I don't trust you or anyone you know. You can visit your family, but you can't take Joy." He wouldn't even care if Joy slept beside my side of the bed in her cot. She would wake up and cry. His eyes weren't the same. It was like he wasn't the man I knew anymore.

After incidents like this, I couldn't go back to sleep. I had to get up for work in a few hours and act like nothing had happened. This would be a regular occurrence. John spent a lot of time on his laptop and tablet nonstop. He would stop to eat and shower, but he was on devices 24/7. He said it was work/study. He really thought I was that stupid. I knew full well he was sitting there looking at all kinds of weird things. He saw conspiracy everywhere, either by the Illuminati, paedophiles, or Satan; it was pure evil. Sometimes I would get home from work and open the door to a smoke-filled flat. He'd burn sage around the flat, calling me Satan. I would find myself crying in the building hallway because I could not breathe, and my eyes were so itchy and red from the burning sage. I asked him to stop doing it because it wasn't normal behaviour. He replied that I was a Satan.

One day, around her birthday, Joy developed a fever and high temperature. I did everything the hospital told me the last time she had a high temperature. Only this time, something was not right. Joy was sleeping in the

49

same bedroom as me. I woke up and saw she was shaking and had bubbles coming from her mouth. I screamed for John to help, and he saved her life that night, giving her first aid while I was on the phone to the emergency ambulance. When I close my eyes, I can still see Joy on the floor, not breathing; I still see her in the hospital bed wired to monitors. When she eventually woke, the doctor told us she was okay, and thankfully there was no damage to the brain. John had saved her that night. Which I will be forever grateful for.

After speaking to the Doctor, John got up and informed me he was going home. It was still very early in the morning, and as he left the room, I broke down, looking at the door as it closed, thinking to myself, How is this normal? Your little girl nearly died, and you go home to get some sleep. I am not moving from here. It devastated me when I needed him the most. He was once again thinking of himself.

The Doctor noticed how upset I was and talked to me. I couldn't hold on to the heart-breaking feelings anymore. It was impossible to hold back the tears. Sobbing, I told the Doctor about how John had treated me, that he'd slapped me a few times on the face, and how he spoke to me. The Doctor said he had a duty to report what I told him.

After the hospital stay, a social worker arranged for a health visitor to visit our home because I confessed to the Doctor. John went mad! He threatened to take Joy away if I didn't sort it. I was so scared! So I told the health visitor the slap was just a one-off, and we argued like other couples. I had a regular home visit from a health visitor. She gave me a domestic abuse card to use if I needed it.

John used this situation to be nasty again.

He told me off for leaving Joy at the hospital alone with the nurse if I needed the toilet or if some nurse gave me a first aid lesson. I wasn't aware that the fever incident was common with little ones, so I needed all the help I could get.

I was so drained by all this; it was like a terrible dream. When I told him about the social worker, he went mental. I told him a few times that he couldn't treat me like that; it was abuse, and he could go to prison for how he treated me. I asked him to seek help. It's not normal what he says and does. He told me I was the one that needed help, not him. That I think I am special or better than him. 'This is not a TV soap program, this is a life', that was his reply. If I told him I would leave first, he would say go; no one is stopping you. Then he will turn back and tell me, 'don't come running back to me; you think you'd find someone else to put up with you, you crazy bitch. I will destroy you and make sure you never see Joy again, and I will have you deported. Your plan to get a British passport is not working, is it?' I got these same constant rants from him all the time.

After the horrible experience with Joy, I always slept next to her. That was when I could get to sleep because of everything happening. At work, I was trying to cover up the bruises, not just those on my face. Some of the girls knew me well and noticed something wasn't right. Sometimes, someone would find me crying in the office or rushing home. I never made it to any girls' evenings or birthdays. I always excused myself. It was like being in prison again.

I was a little scared to travel after what happened with Joy, so I won't see my parents this summer. When I mentioned it to John, his reply was, 'are you so fucking stupid?'. I knew this was not normal, it had to stop, but somehow, I kept finding an excuse. There is madness, and then it calms down into a happy timeline for a while, and then the madness returns like a vicious circle. When you believe it is getting a little better, it hits again. So, the reality is that the relationship just no longer exists.

Everything would be getting worse by the day. Weekly arguments went daily, with now absolutely zero help from John with the household or Joy. Family time didn't exist. Slowly, it was like living with a house mate you cook for, clean for and sometimes have sex with, but even that connection was long gone. I didn't care anymore. I couldn't stand him touching me after he hit or kicked me. And there were days when I missed him, not the person he is now, but from years back, the one I fell in love with. The man I foolishly believed was my best friend, who used to make me smile and would never use a bad word. The one that used to support my dreams, not laugh at my dyslexia or other not-so-perfect details about me. No one is perfect; you accept your partner's habits and help them overcome their insecurities. That's what genuine love is.

A few times in the night, I would wake up, and he was not at home - John had two phones and always turned them off when he was home. When I asked him about him not being home, the answer was always the same 'it's not your fucking business'.

There were no Birthday or Christmas celebrations. He didn't care about anything. I did; I wanted to make them memorable for Joy, but he would not buy one present for her. In his head, it was nonsense. Christmas is for morons and pagans, he'd say as he ran down the hallway to put my little Christmas tree in the trash. I understand you shouldn't spoil your child, but she is the only baby and our only child. What's wrong with wanting to have a special time and make special memories for her? I didn't grow up with a silver spoon in my mouth, but my family always made those moments special, and that's what you never forget. It's about making an effort, not about how much is spent or what is under the tree.

I remember he brought me flowers and chocolates after one of his attacks. My cheek and my ear were sore and red, and I wore a lot of makeup to cover it up and wore my hair in such a way to cover my ear. He didn't apologise or anything. He just left the flowers and chocolates on the kitchen table. It was a difficult time, both physically and emotionally.

I kept trying to save something impossible to save, so I turned John's voice off inside my head when he was shouting. I assumed he must have mental health issues; listening to but not hearing his taunts stopped him from triggering me.

We should support each other in good and bad times, but this is worse than bad. I was torn between thinking, 'You can't leave him. He had no one else! And then Joy, you can't do this to Joy. She needs a family.' and 'Where would I go?' He said many times that he would destroy me if I left; he would take Joy away from me.'

Right. have a brief break, please; this is a lot to take in.

I tried my best to help him. I just couldn't cope anymore. Joy saw things she shouldn't have seen. She is just a little girl.

This interview is not getting any easier, but I have to get this to the end for Joy I had to.

With this paedophilia accusation, sorry, but I have to ask, did you do anything to Joy?

No, never such sick stuff. I do not know why he kept going on about this paedophilia. Honestly, I do not know what was going through his head. The only thing I can think is that he'd got mixed up with something at University, some kind of cult, or maybe it's through watching too many YouTube videos. Watching all those conspiracy theories and Illuminati videos have somehow influenced his sense of reality and made him ultra-suspicious of everything and everyone. Not I, or any of my family members or friends, ever did such sick things that he is so obsessed about.

If Joy misbehaved, I would gently tap her bum to calm her down. I have never put my fingers in her bum, as John has said. Also, when she was potty training, I had to ensure she was clean down there to avoid infection. I don't know what else I can say. Please do what you must, but I am not a paedophile, which is a false accusation from his side. He knew very well Joy was my universe and, as he always said, he would destroy me if I ever left or reported him.

I wondered why he was so obsessed with all this paedophilia stuff. I told him he couldn't speak to people like this and suggested seeking mental help. But he would always twist this against me, saying It's me that is crazy, not him. He always called me a terrible mother, even though I had done nothing wrong. I am the one looking after Joy. His help comes from taking Joy to the nursery twice a week and picking her up once weekly. But he hasn't even done that for months. He sits at home on the computer 24/7, never offering to help or pick her up, so I don't have to rush from work. He would not even watch Joy if I had to go to doctors for anything myself, and there was certainly no way he would take her to doctors when she was ill. His answer would always be: 'you are her mother; sort it out; I don't have time for your shit'.

Whenever myself or Joy was poorly with a cold or cough, I would have to take her and go to sleep on the sofa in the living room because Mister would not be able to get his beauty sleep even though I would still have to get up and go to work and take care of Joy plus everything else in the household when not feeling well.

I couldn't take time off during Christmas, so John had to help with Joy. There was no other choice. Still trying to figure out why, but he didn't leave the flat for four days. He didn't take her to the park once, and I returned home to find her running around still in her pyjamas a few times, which she had been wearing the whole day. He would call me to pick up food on my way from work before the shops closed because there was nothing to eat at home. To be clear, the shop was downstairs, two minutes from the flat. He wasn't interested in anything, just himself, surfing the internet, doing his workout, and that was it. This was not the man I knew. When I was on Skype calls with my parents, he became vulgar and paranoid; he would keep telling me not to point the camera at him even though my parents wanted to see Joy. Years before, John was always happy to chat with my family and even attempted to learn Slovak to be polite.'

Have you ever reported any of this?

Not really, Just once, after one of the incidents, I felt I couldn't do this any longer, so I tried to call the police. He took my phone and smashed it on the wall, then threw the phone in the sink and ran water on it. This was the worst thing he could do. The phone was vital to me, and everything was on there, all Joy's photos, contacts, and family stuff. I didn't use a computer, so the phone was my contact with life outside this madness and world.

That night, I had an absolute meltdown. I am Sagittarius, so I always give people a second chance and try my best to say nothing. But when things pile up, it needs to get out. So when he hit me and broke my phone, I did not stand there and let him beat me up. I fought back. In this state, I would cry hysterically and couldn't breathe again, but he was laughing at me, shouting, 'you crazy bitch, doing this in front of Joy, all because of the stupid phone- that'll teach you a lesson, not to try to call the police.'

Another sick thing he would do was record my reactions on his phone, but only after he had hit me or attacked me when I was fighting back. He would then comment on it whilst recording, 'look this crazy bitch what she is doing; she is mental.' And all that kind of stuff, he would always twist everything and try to make me look mad. It is really hard to explain. I have called Victims support once or twice, but I never tried to report him again until the very last event a few days ago. I knew I had to go for Joy because I would eventually die. I feel terrible. I didn't want Joy to grow up in this toxic environment. She has already seen a lot more than a toddler should see. Seeing this in everyday life is not normal.

She had also hit me a few times and thrown a tablet at me. She doesn't like it when I say 'No, you can't have it' or simply 'No' to something; she screams, shouts, scratches herself, and kicks and behaves like a brat. But then again, I've seen much worse behaviour by other kids in the shops, so I guess it is her age and her environment. She is my entire world, and she deserves a normal life with friends and happiness around her, not two grown-ups in a prison-like relationship with a daddy that tells her that no one can be trusted and who keeps her family away from her.

When Joy would have one of her meltdown moments, instead of him stepping in and helping. He would say, 'what the fuck is going on? What are you doing to her? Joy. what is mummy doing to you?' Last few months, it was always, 'what does mummy do to you? What are you doing to her? Why are you closing the bedroom door? What are you doing in there? He would be up the entire night. I needed to put Joy to bed and get some sleep, as I had to go to work in the morning. I would close the bedroom door so that we could sleep without noise and lights, but then he would come and open them while going on about the paedophilia stuff and verbally abusing me. I have never told anyone about this because I am so ashamed that I was with him for so many years and couldn't help him.

If people heard some of the things coming out of his mouth, they wouldn't believe that he is for real. Or presume he's on drugs or mentally ill. He was quite a smart man who could turn on the charm when he wanted to. A few times, he was very disrespectful to me in the street or in shops, the way he spoke to me. It was like I was his slave or servant. He would tell me, 'you white people, you are all racist'. He keeps talking about history and saying that my family and I are the same. There was no point talking to him. What happened years ago has nothing to do with me.

He would always try to find something to blame on me. One day he was getting ready for university or god knows where and was ironing his jumper. He always made sure he looked sharp and very well dressed and went that extra mile to look after his hair and skin. I was sitting on the sofa, and Joy was playing on the floor. I can't remember exactly what I said to him, but as he put away the ironing board, he took the iron and walked toward me. He says something like, 'You're pissing me off', and puts the iron close to my face. The iron was hot. I could feel the iron heating up my face. It was maybe one or two centimetres from my nose. I stared at him, thinking, is he going to do it? Is he going to burn my face? It terrified me. Everything was happening inside my head, and tears poured down my cheeks. Then, he just walked away and, soon after, left the flat. I just held my lovely little girl in my arms, hugging her. I knew this had to end. Somewhere inside me, there was this secret hope. Maybe after he finishes university, it will all return to normal. I kept trying to make excuses. He is just going through a bad time. Perhaps he was involved in something at the university. I knew that was no excuse for abuse. Millions of people study, work and take care of their families. He does nothing at home, and I don't believe he works anymore.

A lovely woman always said hello to me at the park, in the elevator or on the street. Once when we were chatting, I realised she lived in the flat above ours. She must have heard something of concern, maybe a conversation or sounds coming from our flat. She gave me a look that said, 'perhaps we should get coffee sometime if you feel like talking to someone.'

It looks like there is a lot you have gone through in the last few years. I understand that you most likely forgot something. Now please try your best and recall the last event that made you finally run away from the situation. But this time, try to remember as much detail as you can. Can you do that for me? have some water. I know this is difficult for you.

I am exhausted and feeling sick to the stomach. My thoughts are all over the place, all those years of unhappy incidents that I need to put in order. After some more water, I try my best to control my emotions.

John knew very well I was getting excited about the summer holidays. I wanted to see my parents, as I hadn't seen them in a long time. My brother had bought a little kid's jeep for Joy to drive in the garden. She would love running around picking up fruit and vegetables in the garden and feeding the chickens.

I planned to buy tickets a little in advance, which would be cheaper. A tiny voice in my head told me he would try something to prevent me from seeing my parents again.

It was a typical Wednesday, nothing unusual and after work, I picked up Joy from the nursery and got home. Joy had a little meltdown because someone pressed the button on the bus and then again in the elevator… why do kids like pressing buttons? I knew she was tired after nursery, so it was just this time when she would get upset about stuff like that. I let her buzz the door in the main hallway so she could talk to daddy on on the intercom. Then she would run to him, all the way to our flat as sometimes he would wait for her at the end of the hallway by our door. He seemed to be in an excellent mood and even cooked dinner. I couldn't remember when was the last time he cooked. We had a lovely dinner of ackee and saltfish. It was a pleasant surprise to come back home and have dinner waiting. He was even joking with me, bringing along my dinner; he put a tiny little of his mum's special hot sauce on my fork. My face went red in seconds, just like in a fire. He was giggling back in that kitchen, asking if I was okay. I was like, look, you can't give this to Joy. This is pure fire, man. By now, he was laughing and told me he only put a bit on my fork to see my face. Which for sure worked well.

After dinner, he took his laptop and went to the bedroom. Joy and I were in the living room. Her dinner was still on her small table; she hadn't eaten yet. From one minute to another, she cried about some drawing from school and was getting quite upset. I told her, 'look, honey, and the teacher didn't give me anything, so you may have left it at the nursery. We can look in the hallway for your backpack, okay?'. While looking for the backpack in the hallway, Joy was getting increasingly upset. Sometimes she would scratch her face, so I would hold her arms and try to calm her down. John was on his phone in the bedroom when he came out with, 'what the fuck are you doing to her? What is happening?'

I try to explain, but there is no point he went to get his sage. I took Joy in my arms and walked to the living room, hugging her while he smoked bloody sage around Joy and me. Somehow she calmed down for a moment, so I went to sit on the sofa and had Joy in my arms, gently tapping her on her bum to calm her down again as she started again about the drawing. John returned to the living room and again started on me. 'What are you doing to her? Joy, what does mummy do to you? Does mummy put her finger in your bum?' He keeps doing this. This is not the first time. Then he called me a paedophile again, and I shouted at him and told him to stop this, stop abusing me! Then he took his phone out and recorded me; I have had enough of this abuse now I am trying to get the phone away from his hands, but he keeps recording and calling me all kinds of things, making Joy cry and me shouting at this stage.'

I'm distraught. I am trying not to cry. 'He started to pack his laptop, telling me I am a paedophile, and he is taking Joy to his mums. I am getting agitated now, telling him he wasn't taking Joy anywhere, over my dead body, he is free to go where he wishes, but my little girl is going nowhere. I got up from that side of the sofa to sit away from him and get Joy. He walked forward to me and hit me on the face a few times, and then he kicked me in the stomach. I fell back on the sofa and halfway on Joy's table. Her food went all over the place. Joy was crying and shouting at Daddy. He grabbed Joy in his arms and went to the bedroom while she cried and shouted Daddy. I am following him, yelling,' you are not taking Joy anywhere; do you not understand that?'. He keeps slapping the door on me, calling me names and telling me to fuck off and stop following him into the bedroom.'

Oh, hold on, I forgot to hold on; something was between. I am sorry, my head is everywhere.

It's okay, have a drink and a brief break.

When he kicked me into the living room, I escaped to the bedroom on to the bed. He followed me, sat on top of me, then took his belt off and tied my hands together. As he walked away, he kept calling me names. Joy was in the living room crying. I freed my hands. Then jumped up from the bed and ran behind him. I was still holding his belt in one hand, so I hit him on his back with it. I asked him, 'Who do you think you are to abuse me like this? Do you think I will stand here and let you abuse me like that? You are not normal John; what's happened to you? You need to seek help; you are ill!' John then turned and looked at me. He was furious because I'd hit him back, and his eyes went mad. I turned around and tried to get out of the living room and back into the bedroom because he was becoming more aggressive. In the struggle, I fell over and landed on top of the plastic nappy box, hurting my ribs, and this was when he kicked me in my stomach—now laying breathless, half on Joy's bed, half on the broken box. I didn't feel any pain. I tried to breathe normally and get up so he didn't take Joy away. As I went to the living room, he was face-timing his mum. He didn't speak to her that often. He was telling her all these lies and calling me a paedophile, which made me even more upset. 'Why are you lying to your mother?' He kept on calling me mental and telling his mum how crazy I was.

Joy said she was hungry, so I went to the kitchen to sort out some soup for her. There was a mess all over the flat. He was walking around with his phone talking to his mum; I was following him, he kept calling me names, and I kept telling him, 'why don't you tell your mum the truth about how you are treating me and that you are not well in your head. You can't do this to people. Are you aware this is serious abuse?' he then closed the door in my face. I was still behind the door talking to him about the abuse and his mental health. Then he opened the door and punched me straight in the eyes. For a second, I couldn't see anything. I went dizzy. I could feel my face glowing, and my eyes were very blurry. Looking in the mirror with horror, I saw a huge black and blue eye growing right before me. As tears poured down again, my cheeks and eyes were on fire. I went to the kitchen to get some frozen peas. Joy had eaten her soup, and we both went to the bedroom. I hugged my little girl in my arms, crying; he came again with his phone recording. I keep crying, telling him to leave us alone and get lost.'

Now I am crying. A police officer was looking at me.

Have you seen a doctor with your bruises and where he kicked you?

No, I didn't. I couldn't get out anywhere. There was no chance because he was always home after that incident. I felt no pain until two days later when I lifted Joy to carry her in my arms, running to the train station. I took pictures of what I could, emailed them to myself, and deleted them from the phone. I was Googling all about domestic abuse stuff a year ago and got some tips and advice about recording injuries discreetly. I came to the sad conclusion that I would have to keep some evidence if the worst came to worst. I have saved some pictures of abusive text messages from when he was texting me when I was at work or late from work and some pictures. Not from all the events that have happened, I didn't manage that. And just to be clear, I am not a paedophile.

I didn't say you are. You have done the first step. I know it isn't easy, but it is a start. This last event happens on Wednesday evening, but you didn't leave until Tuesday next week, it's that right?

Yes, that is correct. I didn't know what to do. I knew I had to do something. He was due for an operation on that Friday for a hernia. I was supposed to pick him up at the hospital. Thursday, he went out somewhere for a couple of hours apparently to get some essentials for the hospital, and returned with a Primark shopping bag.

Whilst he was away, I tried to put some documents together. I usually keep everything in one folder, but Joy's passport and birth certificate were missing. At that moment, I knew this was not safe anymore. He might run off with my little girl, or something terrible may happen. I picked up my phone, dialled the number for my Slovak friend Mima, and briefly told her what had happened. Knowing now, I had to tell someone if something happened to me. Tomorrow, he should be at the hospital. Looking to get all those documents together, maybe I could finally get a few things and go somewhere to a hotel, just away from him. My passport and birth certificate were there, but Joy's were missing.

I felt anxious and ashamed to leave the flat with my face like that. My eye was horrendous, and my face was very sore. Strange enough, I didn't feel any other pain at this point.

He left very early on Friday but to my surprise, he returned home later that morning with a hospital bracelet on his wrist, complaining about the NHS as they cancelled his operation. I just looked up and nodded my head. I thought, 'does he think I am a total idiot? If I had had to pick him up from the hospital, It would be evident with all the bruises all over me that questions would be asked, and he could get arrested. After the operation, he would have to stay at home in bed for a while, and that would be hard for him to control me or do whatever he was planning to do with Joy's documents. I felt so sick in my stomach every time I looked at him. As Sunday came, there was no food in the house. John didn't seem to care much about food. I had no choice but to put my sunglasses on, even though outside was grey and rainy. I did my best to cover my bruises, but unfortunately, makeup can only do so much.

I asked him to watch Joy for a few minutes while I ran downstairs to get some food. As usual, he was playing on his phone, sitting behind the kitchen table. His chair blocked my way to the kitchen drawers, where we kept the shopping bags. I politely asked him to excuse himself so that I could get a bag. As I looked over his shoulder, I saw a picture of some girl on his phone screen. Automatically

I asked,' who is that in the photo'? He just gave me one of his 'it is none of your fucking business, bitch!' looks.

Without saying a word, I walked out the door to get some food, feeling warm tears pour down my cheek as I put sunglasses on. I dialled my friend Mima. This was over. There was no chance for us, no hope, no respect. Whatever we had died a long time ago.

The next day I took my passport, birth certificate, home office documents and Joy's red book with me to work. I Had to hide them in different parts of my handbag. It was the hardest day of my life, but with the support of my friends, colleagues and Police, we planned a safe way out of London.

That last night I asked him if he would like to give me Joy's passport back as I noticed it wasn't where I kept it. He looked at me with those eyes, the ones I didn't recognise any longer.' You really are crazy, are you? Don't you get it? You are not taking Joy anywhere, you fucking paedophile!'

That night I wasn't able to close my eyes. How are things coming to an end like this? Why? We were supposed to get married one day and be together happily forever; how was this possible? What's happened to him? What's happened in that university? A million questions were in my head while I was watching him sleep. Knowing this would be the last time I was in the same bed with him. After ten years of being together. Naturally, I reach out for his hand, but he moves his hand away from me and turns to the other side of the bed.

You did well, okay, it's the first step. It is tough for you, but you did the right thing. It is enough for today. Get some rest, and if you recall anything that you forgot. Write notes.

* * *

The Police drove me back to the restaurant. My little angel Joy had a great time with the girls at the kid's play area. Running to me, she said, 'Mummy, I like it here. I had ice cream and lots of other food.' She loves being around people and having someone to play with, not just mummy, all the time.

Miranda was walking forward to me.' Well, how did it go? Let's get you sorted. We are going to town to get you both something to wear and change your phone number.'

We were in the shopping precinct when Miranda's phone rang with disturbing information. John was at her place looking for me! He asked about Miranda and where I was and told people I had run away with his daughter. He was still waiting in a car park with someone in the car. Forget the clothes; Miranda grabbed Joy in her arms and ran with me straight to the nearest Police station. I don't know what I felt at this point, but I knew we were safe with Miranda, and she knew exactly what needed to be done. (everyone that knows her will tell you the same). We spent the next couple of hours at the police station as they couldn't arrest him while waiting for the Metropolitan police in London to respond. After this, the next few days and weeks were pure madness.

The Police arrested John a few days later in London and pressed charges against him. I was talking to police officers, social workers, and domestic abuse support workers now - I didn't know who was who anymore. Some from London, some from Hampshire, some because of Domestic Abuse, some because of his accusations about me being a paedophile. There was no way I could sleep at night. I couldn't eat normally, and whatever I ate would come back out. I can't possibly describe the feelings I had at that time. It was the foundation of everything I was going through and dealing with. Depression, anxiety, stress, sadness, loss, pain, disappointment, feeling ashamed, broken-hearted, insecurity ... I am so lucky to have my little girl and friends around me. I would not be able to make it without all of them.

Next, the hardest step was to tell my parents the truth. Mum wasn't able to stop crying, and daddy was angry. Then nursery, my work and other things needed to be sorted, from which I received substantial support. A colleague went with the Police to our flat. It was a mess. John had taken everything he could, all of his things and whatever was mine, clothes, books, documents, everything that had any value to me. He had left nasty messages on the kitchen cabinets about me, again more stuff, paedophile, but that was nothing new.

I knew I had to stay strong, but this was too much. I was very grateful for Miranda, the girls, and everyone who had rallied around us. There was no way I would cope without them. I didn't realise how bad I was until I saw the size of the clothes Miranda got for me. They were size 4, two sizes down from the regular size I wore. I'd lost that much weight in two weeks.

At night watching Joy sleep, her little smile and tiny hands holding mine gave me the strength to fight and never give up! Even the unbearable pain inside me was something I couldn't get rid of. I don't hate him. I am just really disappointed and hurt. We were together for ten years. It has been a long time, a decade. Every stupid love song or any song that would remind me of him, happy memories would pop out. Oh God, would I ever be all right?

I was far from ready to return to London. I didn't want to return to the flat. They set a court date for October. It was a long time to wait, but they had to gather evidence, reports and interviews. This whole process is very draining, emotionally and physically. It is a painful and personal process.

My head is all over the place, trying to decide what's next, where to work, Joy, bills, and my whole life—a lot to deal with in such a short time.

It was so lovely to be with friends I met when I first moved to England years ago. Each day was a small slow step back to normality, with the help of my friends pushing me, spending time with me and encouraging me to get back to working a few hours. Lovely memories. Life will go on; some people will return to your life forever, some for a little while, and some of them it is time to leave. But memories, they would stay forever. There is a lesson to be learned in every step you take.

* * *

During the summer holidays, we moved in with my oldest best friend, Alishia, at her new pub in Folkestone. Returning to London was too painful, and the court hearing was still far away. It is best to clear my head, take some time to consider my future and then, after the court hearing, it is time to move on with life. Easier said than done!

Summer next to the seaside is definitely different from London. Surrounded by beautiful nature and the sea will help you heal the soul. Getting lost in positive thoughts cleared my mind of the hard times. It was simply a perfect place for broken hearts and an inspiration, a place to hide away or find a new beginning, discover yourself, and for every soul to recover. Joy had a wonderful time exploring the seaside, collecting seashells, making sandcastles, and trying out lots of different playgrounds.

As the court hearing drew closer, it felt unreal and like a dream. Joy was going through the terrible toddler stage, and the word 'No' from me would turn into crazy tantrums. I found this hard to deal with on my own., It's totally understandable, and she is also going through a confusing time; she was missing her routine, nursery, friends, teachers, and dad. This was killing me inside, but there wasn't much else I could do. Just try my best to move on with our lives. It was a blessing to be surrounded by my friends, who pushed me, tried their best to keep me busy and supported me all the way.

When Joy started school, meeting new friends and returning to a routine helped her behaviour improve. Not perfect, but better. I also needed to learn not to raise my voice when she ignored me but use more firmness in my words. It was time to set up new rules and get her the routine she never had. She knew how to test mummy's patience… but all kids do it to their parents.

I met my friend Jennifer in London to visit the flat. After all that had happened, I didn't want to return there, but I had to. Joy and I walked down the corridor together. I was holding her hand; we stood outside our flat and found the door was unlocked. I pushed the front door, and there were piles and piles of post. I had to push Soo hard to get be able to get inside. Joy ran into the living room, threw herself on her toy box and cried hysterically, 'my toys, I miss you, my toys'!

These were the moments I couldn't get out of my head. It was something that I never, ever want to experience again in my life. I broke down in tears, sitting in the flat hallway in the middle of the enormous pile of post and red envelopes. This was our home, the one we had together as a family. This was not supposed to finish like this. The pain inside me was indescribable, as tears poured down my cheeks like a river; I lifted my head and looked up as Joy walked up to me and told me, 'Mummy, mummy, don't cry; daddy is not here. He will not hit you anymore, mummy, don't cry. I love you, mummy'.

I hugged Joy and said, 'I love you too, sweetie, more than the world. Let us go and get some lunch, and buy some bin bags so we can pack these things up.

Jennifer arrived an hour later with wine, chocolate cake and emotional support, ready for packing, a girls' chat and a sleepover. The flat was quite a mess. He took all my documents, books, portfolios and photos of my family that I can't replace. Everything that had any meaning to me. All my clothes and shoes, Joy's clothes as well. He only forgot one bag with summer clothes that were under the bed. So there was not very much for me to pack. I can't even talk about the fridge and freezer. I did my best to sort it out and ignored the insulting writing on the kitchen cabinets about me. I just took a picture of it and left it there. The next morning, Jennifer took Joy to Battersea park for a few hours as I sorted out the rest of the flat. The memory of the last moments in our flat that evening will always stay in my heart. The place holds so many horrible memories and a few happy ones. The place that was our family home. If only those walls could tell their stories. I still see him at the door smiling. Why do these happy memories pop into my head now? You stupid girl, how could you have loved someone like this? Stop this; let it go. It's over, and he ruined everything. Now, lock this door and your feelings for him there, too. Let them stay here with the belongings that he left. And walk away from the last ten years of your life.

Court Hearing

The court hearing was now just a week away. I wasn't feeling so good. I have had sleepless nights, anxiety and stress for a few days now. The toilet has become my best friend lately, even though I eat very little. There is a vast emptiness and pain inside me, nothing else. Just the thought of seeing him makes me feel sick to the stomach. It is going to be a long few days in court.

The months of waiting for the court case had been tough and emotionally challenging. Now I honestly understand why so many women never report domestic abuse. This was difficult, very personal, and emotional. You need to be very strong to face this, and I knew his Barrister was going to do everything within her power to make me feel I had done something wrong.

How she talked to me shocked and disgusted me, twisting everything I said against me. Saying, 'You this, it is you who did this, it's you, not him!'

As the trial started, I sat in the courtroom, I had been beaten and bruised by John for years, and the thought of him getting away with it was too much to bear. I had hoped that justice would be served, but as his Barrister presented her evidence, it became clear that she was biased towards her client. How could she defend someone who had caused so much pain and suffering? How could she twist the facts to make it seem like he was innocent?

I felt like standing up and screaming, "How can you do this? How can you defend someone who has hurt me so much? What happened to girl power?" You should be ashamed of yourself and pray to God that you never experience something like this! I was horrified.

The Barrister even brought my parents into it and made comments such as, 'are you collecting material for your new book?'

On the other hand, I had great legal support on my side. She talked about the years of abuse I had endured, the bruises and black eyes, and the fear that had ruled my life. They spoke about how John had manipulated me and made me feel like I was the one to blame for everything that had happened. The judge was a lovely human with experience and probably a heart in the right place, as well as morals. She was kind and understanding.

My work colleagues and friends were there to support me, although I couldn't speak to them or get comfort during the trial. I was grateful for the victim support team ladies that were there for me the whole time.

She knew. After three hard days in court, she knew I was right. Her hands were shaking while she was reading from her papers as I was so upset, and I answered her accusations passionately.

I stood in that wooden box after enduring years of mental and physical abuse, and I felt like I was being abused all over again! And this was when I realised I needed to do this not just for Joy and me but for every woman who wasn't strong enough to stand up for herself here. Because now I understand how traumatic and hard this is. It's far too personal and emotional, and not everyone is strong enough to hear this abuse again from the legal profession that thinks it is okay to do so!

I understand in our legal system; everyone is entitled to a fair trial. Even if that means those accused of terrible crimes have the right to a competent defence. I know It doesn't mean they condone or excuse their client's behaviour, although I was told he was on his fifth Barrister. He kept changing them. I wonder why?

Every night Miranda and the rest of my friends would check in on me to see if I was all right, and then the girls and Joy would call too. I never left Joy alone for a minute. I knew she was being looked after well, and girls cared for her. They no longer needed me in court except if I wished to stay and listen to his side. 'No, thank you, your honour, I would prefer to go to my daughter if that's all right.'

On my way home, I stopped at my old workplace. The people in my life were blessings. They gave me much-needed hugs, and their familiar faces made me feel better.

The next day, I had a call from my police officer requesting that they needed me back in court the following day for further cross-examination. I am afraid I have no babysitter this time, so Joy had to come with me.

Once again, the defence made me cry as she produced a video that John had made. It was of Joy while he asked her, 'Who does this to you?' and the poor child whispered 'mummy'. What kind of mentally sick person does this? Then another video from a long time ago. I was wearing underwear, holding on to my ribs, as I remember he kicked me a few times. I was crying and wanted to leave. He shouted at me, 'leave your child; you cannot be a mum' while holding Joy. I tried to get his phone from his hands while he kept calling me names.

How low would he go? Can't they see this is not normal? Can't they see he is not right in the head, and they have no problem with that? I couldn't even say one word, nothing, the pain and the reality of something that you know is sickly wrong, and you can't do anything about it. It was unbearable!

Now it is done; I faced him and his lies and that defence barrister. Woman's power kiss my ass, where is it? It is very different being a victim of domestic abuse without having worries about your financial situation on top of everything else. That is one of the many reasons women don't report domestic abuse or leave it until the very last minute. Where do you go? How are you going to take care of your kids all alone? How will you pay bills, mortgages and then your mental health? Many women would need medication or anti-depressant to deal with all this. Not everyone is strong.

A few days later, I was told they had dismissed the court because of a jury problem. One of them had made a racist comment, and another said, 'I used to hit my wife; I don't see a problem with it '.

How is this happening? I don't get it. How do these people get picked? This is madness, and this is the kind of mess who is supposed to decide things that would change your life. What a joke!'

'Ivana, I know this is very upsetting. I promise you; this has never happened before. If you don't wish to carry on, that's understandable.'

Exactly why would you think I would give up now? There is no way I am not doing this anymore, not just for my little girl and me but for every abused woman out there!'

I will update you with the new court date, and in the meantime, you know where we are."

In the following months, some information came to light from his life before we met. He forgot to mention a few salient facts, such as his existing children. Years of being together under one roof, a person you would believe you knew well, was your best friend, and you didn't know him at all.

I remember very well the day we went to sort out Joy's birth certificate. The lady at the registry office asked a simple question" Do you have any other children?" His answer was NO! How could you deny you had children?! What kind of human, not even a father, for sure. I was so angry at myself for loving this man, this liar!!! As time goes on, thanks to paperwork and me trying to sort out life, a few more surprises, money-related, claims will pop out.

I felt sorry for him. He has problems, that's for sure. Would I ever know why? He had everything, family and people around that cared for him. Never mind what has happened in the past; no one was born perfect. But honesty, trust and respect are something that he didn't understand. And that is over for me. He did everything he could to make sure of that. I'd never believe a word that ever came out of his mouth. As for Joy, she needs a father, a role model, not a liar.

* * *

December is a little more complicated this time. It is a family holiday, and this crazy guilt inside me, mixed with loneliness, is not doing me any good. Joy should be having a great time with all her family from both countries, with Daddy and a picture-perfect dream family that didn't work out. I try to cover up my feelings of this reality check- I am a single mother, lonely until I die. These crazy thoughts come along this time of year. Also, my birthday is coming up soon, so like it or not, I'm getting older too. Some of my dear friends suggested that maybe I should go out a bit and move on with life, but the thought of dating, or any new man around me, any man at all, made me feel sick in the stomach. I guess my facial expressions would say it better than words themselves. I have an invisible fuck off sign on my forehead.

The healing process will take a while, and it will take a long time before I can trust anyone again, let alone love someone, let someone into our lives as Joy is my entire world. There is no way on this planet I would let just anyone near us! This is the sad reality of domestic abuse. Bruises fade away. Trauma and pain stay for life, But to love and trust someone again is very difficult, sometimes impossible to repair.

I would love no one again, but I have the most incredible little girl that loves me more than anyone in the world, and that kind of love is unconditional! The love that only a mother would understand. Love that keeps you alive and never lets you give up on anything because never mind how hard your day or, what stage your life is at, what challenges life puts you through. My little angel is there with her beautiful smile running to the school gates shouting "my mummy". And that is pure love and a blessing from God!

So for this year's birthday, we spent time with one of my dearest friends, Adi and her family. We all met up with a few friends in London on the way and even reconnected with special ones I had not seen in many years. Christmas was lovely; I enjoyed the restaurant vibes, taking me back to the good old days of my youth. Joy enjoyed playing Mary in the school nativity play. We all were so proud of her! I found it a little hard fighting tears when I saw all the dads in the audience. John will never get the chance to see how incredible she is. He should be here, involved in all those things.

The seaside town was sleepy during the winter, but it didn't lose its charm even then. I could sit on the beach and stare at the sea forever, lost in my little world. What I didn't enjoy or never got used to were the seagulls. And the freezing winter cold wind.

I was so happy seeing Joy doing well at school and making new friends. Coming out of her shell was helping with her tantrums.

The new year arrived, and with that, a new life for me, for us. I must move on and find a way to make a new life from scratch again.

I remember one day when I was picking up shells with Joy at the seaside. As we walked along, she looked up at me and said, "Mummy, you need to buy a new dress and shoes, blue shoes and pink lipstick, and you need to go to the ball, just like a princess."

I stared at her in shock. "Well, I don't really like Balls, sweetie, maybe not this time, OK."

She looked at me and said." Mummy, but you have to find a new prince. Daddy is not your prince; he didn't want to be your prince ".

My four-year-old girl was talking to me about grown-up stuff. I wanted to cry; I was in shock. What is going on in her little head? Since we left, I didn't care what I wore or how I looked. Leggings, a T-shirt and a long pencil dress were all I needed.

They say that time heals everything. Yes, but a lot of time must pass to heal some of the pain. There were days when he was just in my head, and I kept questioning what went wrong and why. One day, I was food shopping and wrapped up in my little world, walking between the aisles in Asda, when I realised my shopping basket was more or less full of the kind of food he liked. I automatically just put stuff in the basket for him. I suddenly realised I was not in London; I was in Folkestone. Wow, my mind was spinning. I dropped the basket, fighting back the tears. I walked outside the store straight to the beach for a long walk. It was really hard to explain. People wouldn't understand. I had to let it go, not in my head but inside my heart; I have to learn how to forgive him and move on with my life.

It may be time to find myself again and the things I used to love to do. So, I reconnected with a few old friends, including someone who had become very supportive and made me smile occasionally. I realised how many people I had cut off from my past because of John's jealousy.

Joy made a best friend at school called Alise, and I have made a new best friend with her mum. It was also nice to see Joy spending time with other children, and it was lovely for me to meet someone new. Weeks passed by slowly, and the new court date was approaching quickly. This was one part of the process I needed to get on with. After that, I could figure out what was next for us. There were wonderful days when I was thrilled and positive, and there were days when I just wanted to cry into my pillow for a million reasons. Missing London friends, missing my job, missing him (but I didn't know why), and the scary reality that I needed to start again from nothing and alone with Joy.

Second Court Hearing

The court date finally arrived. This time I am the woman that fights for all victims. I tried to dress smartly, wear a little makeup and look like a woman who has pulled herself together and fought for this cause! I am stronger than his lies and abuse. I would do my utmost not to cry. I will speak up and stand up for myself. Not just for myself but for those who never got the chance to stand up there, even if I must do it for the second time.

Once again, we had updates. One minute he is pleading guilty; the next minute, not guilty. This is like a never-ending saga.

I was trying my best to be strong and had been preparing myself for months not to cry or get upset, so that morning, on my way to the court, I was smiling. I had the support of people around me, plus someone a little special who helped me build myself up—helped me to see myself and my values and that when I get to court, I am there as a survivor, not a victim, because he can't walk over me anymore! He could see what he had, and he didn't appreciate it.

I notice John has another new Barrister. What a surprise! It looks like the last one gave up or finally realised all was not right.

This Barrister was quite a nice-looking older man. He had a kind look when he noticed me outside in the hallway. Still, I knew he would give me a hard time in there, so I didn't feel like sharing a kind smile with him.

I always hate the uncomfortable silence in court before the jury comes in. I tried my best to avoid eye contact or even look at John. It was a horrible feeling to be so close yet so far away in life. He looked tired and not well. He has a beard like a bloody goat now too. Not cool, man; what are you thinking? And why am I even thinking about this? Stop it right now, these silly thoughts! Why do lovely memories keep coming back to me? This is the opposite of what I've been preparing for months!

That's it now, I thought, don't look at him at all. Just remember all the lies he told, how he used you, disrespected you and broke your spirit! Now pull yourself together at once! Focus, woman, focus!

You can prepare as much as you like, but emotions and feelings are stirred when faced with reminders of the years of abuse and lies again, and it isn't easy to control the tears. I was much better than last time, that's for sure. His Barrister still challenged me, but not like the previous one. His approach was different, not as abusive as hers. He didn't ask about stuff that had nothing to do with the case. He tried to suggest things and twist things like she did last time. I would answer the same way, 'No, it wasn't like that … it happened like this …'.

This time the jury asked questions, which made me feel better because they were paying attention. It was still a hard few days in the court. It was a very emotional experience, no matter how strong you are. How much can you take as a human being? Some lies that came out from his side were so hurtful and quite shocking. At one point, they had to call a break and take me out as I got distraught. He said he had been trying to get rid of me for years.

I screamed with tears pouring down my face. You were sleeping with me, you liar; no one was holding you if you wanted to go!'

His Barrister asked, 'My client said he didn't have an intimate relationship with you.

"No, that's lies", I reply.

He kept asking me the same question until the judge saw I was upset and called the break saying, 'I believe Miss Ivancakova answered your question already. There is no need for this!'

I was so grateful for the Victim Support ladies who took me away from there to calm down. I was shaking, the bloody cheek of it. He was most likely cheating on me all those years. I have to calm myself down before I make myself ill.

Every evening I would check on the girls and Joy. Then my friends would check on me, and one special one would check a few times during the day and call in the evenings to calm me down and help me into a positive mindset.

* * *

On the last day of the court hearing, they called my colleague in to give evidence, although I couldn't speak to her. As I watched Shy give her evidence, it was horrendous, and she cried while answering. I watched her sit with the Victim support lady and cry with her. John's Barrister was horrible to her, twisting everything against her answers. Once again, speculating and suggesting, it was difficult to watch. Until now, I wasn't aware of how many girls would notice, and they knew things weren't right in my personal life. The bruises, my excuses to never attend any girl's evenings out, all those little things they noticed. She burst into tears when asked to describe me as a person, mum, and ex-colleague.

That week in court was very draining, emotionally and physically. How much more would he hurt me? How many more secrets and lies are there? Do I want to know anymore? No, it's not going to change anything. John knew me well. What hurts the most was that he had been my universe, my best friend. He knew everything about me. As a Sagittarius, if you lie to me, it's straightforward. I am finished with you because whatever comes out of your mouth, I can't trust. Someone that was in your life for that long is not just a broken friendship and trust, but it's love you betrayed. At some point, I hoped I would wake up, and this was just a terrible dream, and all this had never happened.

I wish I could start again and return to the day we first met outside McDonald's in Stratford. Back to my high heels, huge makeup box and crazy single London life. Why did I have to wink at him? That tiny little thing changed everything in my life! Sitting here, staring at the witness box, Shy is still there, and I am in my little world, with my memories and happy flashbacks. All I wanted to do right now was to stand up and walk straight to him, right in front of that glass box where he is sitting and ask him only one question. WHY?

Finally, I was free to go home. My legal team would let me know what was next, and I was very grateful for all their support. I am not the easiest person to work with; you need to be patient and have answers to my questions. If there is no answer or you don't know. I would find out myself. This had been ongoing for nearly two years. In that time, the police saw me crying, shouting, asking questions, demanding, frustrating, and finding the courage to stand up for myself. I had a lot of patience and never gave up on what was right. Also, the victim support team at the court were terrific; those ladies are volunteers and make a vast difference to the victims. I was so grateful that someone was always there for me when I couldn't speak to my friends or legal team for emotional support. Those are little things in people's lives that make a tremendous difference. Kindness doesn't cost money.

Many victims never report their experiences for many reasons, and you can't judge people because it takes time and courage to do so. Most times they have no support with no one to turn to or when children are involved and financial situations. Sadly there will always be huge reasons women don't seek help until the last minute, if even that. So once again, a sad reality of this world is the power of money. It is time to change that, speak up and make a difference because everyone can do good things in life and be kind and respectful to each other.

* * *

It was time for coffee and some brunch. Finally, I could talk to Shy. It has been an endless week, a difficult time. I have missed London, my friends, work, and park visits.

Before going to King's Cross station to catch my train back to Folkestone, I stopped to meet a few friends—a few work colleagues and someone who had been a substantial support all this time. Whatever happens from now on, I have done what I set out to do, two court cases to fight for my human right to live a happy and fulfilled life without loss, harm or fear from people.

No one should have to accept living as someone's slave with no opinions, feelings, ambitions or dreams. To be looked down on and annihilated isn't love.

I missed my little Joy terribly, even though I spoke to her on the phone every day. She has probably had a great time with the girls and our new friends. A week away from her, it's far too long for me.

Nothing in the world made me happier than seeing Joy's smile as she ran towards me at the train station. Today she was with her new best friend Alice and her mum, my new mummy friend. When she kissed me and said, 'Mummy, I love you so much, I have missed you! 'nothing mattered more than that.

No one ever knew what was happening behind closed doors. From the outside, we might have looked like a perfect couple with an ideal life and perfect family. Many times it's all just a cover-up. The sad reality is that it is happening to you, not anyone else. It is not a soap opera. Children are the innocent ones who witness the madness and tension. One thing I will always regret is that I didn't leave sooner. Joy has seen a lot, and it has affected her. It is a tough decision to make to save a family or save yourself and a child. That's why women should stand up, speak up and raise awareness of domestic abuse.

The Verdict

I received a phone call from a Police Officer around a week later that I had been waiting for for a very long time. They found John guilty of domestic abuse, Bodily harm and a toxic intimate relationship. Finally, it came to an end.

John was sentenced to three and a half years imprisonment and given a restraining order. The judge told him off for manipulating and using Joy with these paedophile videos. The Police Officer asked how I was feeling. Honestly, I wasn't sure how I felt. A part of me was happy that it was over and I could live my life again. And another part of me felt so sad inside how it all ended. I didn't want this to happen; I didn't want him to go to prison. If he had just listened and sought help, the outcome could have been better. It's down to John to accept the facts that others can see until he realises that no one can help him but himself.

I did the best I could. I gave him everything I had to give over our ten-year relationship. Then I looked at the phone in my hand. There were a few people I wanted to speak to. But first, there was one person who I needed to call first.

It was time to move on with our life now; we can't live on hold like this forever. As the weeks passed, we enjoyed the seaside as much as possible. It is a healing and wonderful place to raise a family or retire. But we needed to move on with our life. We needed a home, a new start, and a peaceful life. Joy needed routine and her own bedroom. Work was calling me. London felt like my proper home. It made me feel more independent as a woman than a single parent. I knew it would not be easy, but nothing in my life was.

We had met some lovely people, made some good friends, and learned some new skills, too; I'd spent time with my oldest friends, and Joy got to know them too. Miranda, Lesley and the girls are like the family that is there for you. Both of us have had time to recover and spend precious time together. Life might change a few things; people move on in different directions, and their minds have different opinions, but they always are your family. That is a unique gift to find, and we have kept that kind of friendship for many years. I may never have been lucky in love, but life has blessed me with people in my life that are just like my family.

When Joy finished her first year at school, we flew off to see her grandparents in Slovakia.

This was much-needed time with my family and a return to that simple village life on the farm. Joy enjoyed herself in the garden, running around and picking up fruit and vegetables. She hardly spent any time indoors and loved having barbecues every day, having dinner outside on the patio, playing with her dolls, and sitting in her little tent and her jeep. She loves driving as far as the battery lasts every day.

I met some friends from college and caught up with my cousins and their little bundles of joy.

It was so good to have my mum around. I needed that, yes, we regularly spoke on Skype, but that is different. She was heartbroken by the whole situation. She even kept praying for John.

Starting a new life

We moved back to London before September so Joy could start the term at her new school, and I would be back at work as soon as possible. Life never goes to plan, but having one and trying to follow it is better.

'Mummy, do we have to move again, mummy? Her eyes were glistening. She had such a big smile. I don't want to go to another house again and to a new school. Can't we stay here? I have my room just like a big girl. Because I am not a baby anymore. I love our new home. It is lovely, and I can play anywhere I like.

'We are not moving again, at least not for a while. I am thrilled you love this place and your new school. I love you so very much. Never forget that!'

We had managed to get ourselves a lovely place to settle into, thanks to the support of friends, my employer, Refuge, Victim support, the school and the rest of the people involved. Maybe not with all the furniture we needed. We had what we had for a new beginning.

After the crazy times, we could enjoy our first Christmas in our home and even had a few friends around for a holiday. Joy had her best friend Alise with my new best friend, her mum, around for a weekend, and of course, we showed them a London Christmas Wonderland.

This was a new chapter in our lives, the better one, the one that would let us make only happy memories, the moments that we will cherish for life and never-ending love. Nothing is more important than seeing my little Joy smile, happy and settled in her new school and having a new happier adventure.

As usual, I am super-extra tired as everything is always challenging. Nothing in life comes easily. A single, working mum must be on top of their organisational skills and superpowers. Plus, the essentials, coffee, chocolate and huge sunglasses to cover those tired makeup-free face. I am not saying it is easy; it's not; it's exhausting. Work, school, half terms, activity clubs, and holiday clubs juggled around the school timetable.

But it is possible. I have become myself again. I've managed to write again at long last despite my lack of confidence being dyslexic. I hope my words will inspire women to make the first steps to a new future and a safe life before it is too late. To fight for your beliefs, happiness, love, and peaceful life. A life where you can give your opinion out loud, a life where you can work in a job you love. A Life where you can talk to people and have a social life without being abused mentally and physically on a weekly basis. A Life without the sick feeling in your stomach every time you put the key in the door.

Rebuild confidence in yourself because you are who you are, you are perfect in your way, and you are a strong woman to finally get the courage to stand up for yourself and make your life for who you are. Not for what someone had made you become.

Time heals everything. We move on and forgive but never forget. I'd be lying if I said things are perfect now. There are days when I feel so lonely and tired of everything, days when Joy asks for a baby sister or a new daddy. Days when I don't have answers to her questions. Days when she gives me a hard time, days when I want to cry and I can't sleep at night because I can't balance the finances, or even because a silly song has reminded me of him. This is life and reality, not a movie. And life comes with difficulties with feelings, problems and challenges. It's okay to cry and moan, then pull yourself together and get on with it. Never give up because someone tells you, you can't do it, or you are not good enough. You never know what you can do if you never try it.

As for John, he is now out of prison on probation, but unfortunately, he didn't change. Naively, somewhere inside me, I was hoping for him to change, to learn a lesson. To get help and maybe try to make things a little normal and human for Joy. My dream was to become a normal separated parent and to move on with our lives positively. Well, it didn't work like this. He seems to believe in his own world, that he thinks he has done nothing wrong, and it's me who is the crazy one who made up the case against him with the help of the officials involved.

Sadly, I still experience his abuse on social media. He uses fake profiles to abuse me online, calling me a paedophile and tagging me with celebrities connected with this issue. He keeps calling Social Services and reporting me for being a paedophile. So having this continued abuse again and dealing with that isn't easy. It's time for me to put all the pleasant memories of him in a box and bury them. I did everything I could to help him, but he won't let go. It's his choice to ruin his life, and he has lost people that genuinely cared for him. Once trust has gone, it's gone. Be a man, take responsibility for your actions and accept your mistakes. Negativity, lies, cheating, using people, and toxic energy will get you back one day. Remember, what goes around comes around. Karma will get you someday.

I haven't given up on finding true love just yet. Even my friends are trying to set me up on dates to move on with life. But we live in a fast-moving world with no responsibility, a lack of commitment and little freedom. Letting someone new into our life is a tremendous step, and after my experience, I will think twice before committing again.

With age and life experience, you become more careful about who you let in your life. I'm not interested in the men out there that are just into looks and social status or having fun with no responsibility. Even after all that I have gone through, I still believe there is true love out there for everyone, even if it takes a lifetime to find it. True love and soul mates always find a way to each other. There is always a reason people come into your life!

Not all love stories finish with a happy ending. That doesn't mean true love doesn't find you.

Love is not something you look for; love is something you feel when it is there!

After many years, I can finally breathe.

THE END.

Acknowledgements

I would like to thank my family back home in Slovakia, my friends, to everyone there for my daughter and me during the most challenging times. You all know who you are.

Those who were there for us from the very beginning, my English family, from my work friends, police, legal team and all the officials involved. As well as support from Refuge, Victim support, school and new friends we have both made.

Also, an incredibly special thank you to David, who always believed in me and pushed me to try to find myself again. For making this book become a reality and for dealing with all, well, me …

Thank you to my little girl for giving me the courage and the strength. I love you more than you could ever imagine.

And finally, Thank you to that Someone who always made me smile without even trying for your support and understanding and, well everything.

Thank you to the lovely and talented Alexandra Tarcinska for the fabulous book cover.

I am incredibly grateful for everyone in my life, and I was blessed to receive so much support from my friends, family, charities, and all the officials.

I hope that authoring this book is not just a way of healing but, most importantly, to inspire those that mind has been in a comparable situation, those that feel trapped, and those that cannot see the red flags or do not want to accept the reality. Or those that feel like no one would believe them, there is nowhere to go to, financial situation or whatever mind be a reason you cannot make a first step toward your freedom. Believe me, it is not easy, but there is help available out there. You are not alone.

I have never said it was easy, but there is hope for a new life for you and your children.

If you or someone you care about is experiencing domestic abuse you can contact:

The National Domestic Abuse Helpline 0808 2000 247
www.nationaldahelpline.org.uk

www.refuge.org.uk   @refugecharity

www.victimsupport.org.uk   @victimsupport_uk

www.womensaid.org.uk   @womesaid

Broken Rainbow Helpline 03009995428

Men's advice line - 08088010327

From international model to international prisoner

SLOVAKIAN
BEST SELLING
NOVEL

Big Girls Don't Cry

IVANA IVANCAKOVA

Also available by Ivana

Her first book *Big Girls Don't Cry*

A true story, from catwalk to prison.Ivana grew up in a small village in Slovakia, thumbing through fashion magazines and dreaming of life as a model. Despite many obstacles, in 2008, she made it to London and began to work her way up in the fashion industry – modelling, booking models, and doing make-up and styling on photo-shoots. She worked hard and made it to be catwalk model for London Fashion Week. The city fashion and club scene was a far cry from quiet village life, and she loved every crazy minute of it: the glamour, the parties, the people…Then she was offered a modelling job that would change her life. She was to be the lead model for a new, exciting collection. She flew out to Buenos Aires, delighted to get international work. However, the whole job was a set-up that cost her two years in a Parisian jail!This book started as a diary that she wrote to help her get through each horrific day behind bars. Her brutally honest and deeply personal account of her rollercoaster journey lays the dangers of the fashion industry bare.

Publisher : I_AM Self-Publishing (5 Dec. 2016)
Language : English
Paperback :184 pages
ISBN-13 : 978-1911079798
Dimensions : 12.7 x 1.17 x 20.32 cm
Also available as an Ebook

available at
amazon

Ingram Content Group UK Ltd.
Milton Keynes UK
UKHW010701100523
421517UK00004B/185

9 781913 898700